Foreword – The Objective

At first glance this book may appear to be nothing more than a compelling and interesting story about my personal experiences. However, that is not the case. Although the book is a consuming story, when I commenced writing it I had several objectives. I simply wanted to share my story with readers, in order for them to know how important it is on all levels of their being, (that is the mental, physical and emotional aspects of themselves) to properly deal with past traumas, in order to be free!

I also wanted to show that it is often the case that one thinks and feels one has dealt with negative issues, only to later find that they have instead been buried deep within their subconscious; and from there are still having power over them and influencing them on a daily basis. In addition, I wanted to illustrate the fact that it is possible to be released from the effects of the lasting trauma, which abuse of any kind enforces upon one and therefore demonstrate the power of the mind.

I decided to share my story, which was not an easy decision to make, in the hope that after reading it, others may be prompted into thinking about their own lives. Also, through sharing with readers my innermost thoughts and feelings, they would gain the strength to examine their own traumas and then work towards freeing themselves. The book tells of my personal struggle and how I found freedom. I know that I am not alone in the struggle to recover from abuse and that millions of men and women the world over have suffered at the hands of another in this way. I also acknowledge that there are many, many techniques, which aid the journey to recovery; however, by sharing my story, I hope to provoke readers to seek freedom for themselves.

Unless one has experienced the powerlessness and vulnerability of abuse, one cannot presume to understand its after-effects. For as the proverb states:

'Ripples continue to form, long after the stone has been thrown into the pond.'

Unfortunately, sexual abuse is a negative aspect of society, a part that has, and probably always will exist. A part that is often swept under the carpet and not spoken about! Sexual abuse is not limited to rape; but includes anything and everything that has a sexual connotation and is undesired by the recipient. There are many reasons why people do not 'tell' of abuse; often victims do not share details of their experience with anyone, as they feel in some way responsible for the actions of their abuser, which of course, is totally unjustified. Many victims feel that if others knew their 'history', they would be judged negatively. Many injured parties feel tarnished and many are afraid to 'tell'. It is time to address this - time for the victims to take control, regain the power and work towards freeing themselves. Therefore, it is my hope that my story will urge people to do just that – seek freedom!

Let the journey commence...and...wherever your journey takes you...may your destination be freedom!

Chapter One

Finding Faye

It was a very hot May afternoon in the South of France and eight of the group who called ourselves The Searchers had just travelled over four hours in a mini-bus for a barbeque with David Bailey and his family. It seemed bizarre to travel so far just for a barbeque with someone that we hardly knew. David had told us it would probably only take an hour and a half from the house we had rented for the week in Laroque near Perpignan. After an hour and a half, still miles from our destination we had passed the point of no return and so continued, wondering why this meeting had been arranged in the first place. We were aware the Baileys were spiritual, as were we, but as the mini-bus rattled on we all knew that something special had been 'set-up' by those above!

Several months earlier, Lindsay, a member of The Searchers group, had been involved in arranging a huge festival of Mind Body and Spirit in Kent. It was an enormous affair with hundreds of spiritual stalls, attended by readers of all sorts and spiritual teachers offering workshops on all manner of spiritual subjects. Many of those taking part had travelled great distances in order to take up the opportunity of being part of the festival.

Annie and Carol, other group members, had decided to go to the festival and it was there that they 'bumped' into David. David was a pianist who, whilst being overshadowed by his spirit helpers, gave recitals of music to audiences on his grand piano. Carol knew David's parents well and stopped to ask after them. During the course of the conversation David had said that he was now living in the South of France. When Annie informed him that The Searchers were soon going to the South of France on holiday, he insisted that we join him and his family for a barbeque.

And so here we were travelling across France on the hot May afternoon in a mini-bus – past the point of no return... The sun hung low in the sky and its heat made travelling uncomfortable. It had now been four hours since the group had set off; we were all thirsty and hungry. Our muscles needed to be stretched and we were beginning to get irritable.

David had been waiting for us as we left the main road, as promised. We followed his Mercedes deep into the French countryside. He was right, we thought, we would never have found the château on our own. Suddenly, David turned off the lane we had been travelling along and sped up a dirt track!

"Where are we going now?" exclaimed Lindsay, who was driving the mini-bus.

Finally, after what seemed like an eternity, David's car disappeared behind a tall hedge. There was no way we could follow, and so we waited, perplexed. Through a thin patch in the hedge we could see a building and a beautiful garden, but no signs of David or his car. After some time, Lindsay started to reverse the mini-bus back down the dirt track. Then a young man appeared through a small gap in the hedge and signalled to us to park in a small lay-by beside the hedge. Lindsay did as instructed and we all gathered our belongings. We were so pleased to have finally arrived and were in desperate need of the bathroom. As the mini-bus doors opened and one by one we stepped out, our mouths fell open in awe- it was like stepping into a piece of heaven! A veritable haven - a sanctuary!

"Wow! What a place!!" we all exclaimed.

The welcome that awaited us in the château was totally overwhelming; the family filed out into the garden at the first sight of the mini-bus and, as the weary travellers alighted we were uplifted by the beaming smiles and generous hospitality offered. The panoramic views from each direction were breathtaking - it wasn't possible to see another building and the views offered only nature at its finest. Within minutes the long, tedious journey was forgotten and the air of tranquility that emanated from this special place reached the souls of each of us.

After refreshing ourselves, we stepped onto the small patio at the rear of the chateau. Again, nature spilled out as far as the eye could see. Green fields, trees, and indescribable perfection. Breathtaking splendour that would make even an atheist question the existence of a superior being. Walking back through the guest annex we stepped onto the main patio. A huge wooden table was set for thirteen - it was reminiscent of the 1990's T.V. programme, 'The Darling Buds of May'. It certainly was a darling place to be and the buds and new blossoms that surrounded the patio reflected the numerous colours of an artist's palette, each with its own pungent aroma. What a wonderful place visit in May. The barbeque was a lavish affair, accompanied by succulent homemade dishes, culminating in an exquisite cherry crumble dessert made with cherries picked that morning from the trees that surrounded the patio.

During the long, lazy meal, the groups exchanged information about themselves and the spiritual pathways we were walking. I explained how The Searchers were a group of people from different walks of life but with one common interest. The group had begun in 1996 because we all shared a thirst for spiritual knowledge and enjoyed searching together for the truth of our existence as well as exploring things seen and unseen!

The Searchers and The Baileys in France

The group members visiting France consisted of me, the leader and teacher of The Searchers. I was in my late thirties and also taught spiritual development and worked as a trance medium.

Annie, my mother, was in her late fifties. She was a healer and loved nothing better than to share her energies with those in need of healing, although she looked forward to the weekly Searchers' meetings where we would sit together and discuss all manner of spiritual subjects.

Sue, who was nearing fifty, worked as a nursery nurse. She, like me, had always had a bond with friends whom others could not see. She knew those from the spirit world were never far away and over the years she had developed the gift of mediumship as well as automatic spirit writing.

Rusty, was in her early seventies and now retired, after having spent her working life as a teacher. She had, for many years harboured an interest in spiritual matters that only now did she have the luxury of the time to explore. Rusty was eager to learn as much as she could about spiritual matters and would have been happier if the group could have met virtually every day!

Thelma, also now retired and of similar age to Rusty, had joined the group at a time in her life when she had been experiencing much emotional turmoil. The Searchers had supported her and put her back together and she had grown and become an important group member, loving all aspects of the work the group did, including channelling healing energy.

Then there was Anne, a year older than Annie. She was a quiet gentle soul, who enjoyed her work as a healer as well as the spiritual learning that the group did together.

Lindsay was the same age as Anne and had been invited to join the group initially when we were studying the effects of food and nutrition on the physical and emotional well-being of a person prior to attending a conference in London entitled 'Living in The Field'. Lindsay was a Nutritionist and Wellness Coach and offered the group a wealth of information on the subject. By the time the conference was over, she had become a part of the group and found she too enjoyed the Spiritual Searching and so was asked to join permanently!

Elaine was the 'baby' of the group, being a few years younger than I but also she was the newest member! She had only joined the group a few months before the trip to France, although she had often assisted me when I was giving Trance demonstrations. Elaine was developing the art of trance mediumship too and loved all aspects of spiritual learning.

A few members of The Searchers Group had stayed at home; Mary had just turned eighty and felt that the trip would be too much for her – however, she still enjoyed the group meetings and discussions as well as meditations, as did the other elderly member of the group who had remained at home - Barbara, a few years younger than Mary.

The final member of the group was Carol. It was Carol who was responsible for setting up the barbeque with David. She had planned to accompany the rest of the group to France but unfortunately, a few days before we were due to set off, she had fallen and broken her foot and with it in plaster poor Carol realized, much to everyone's disappointment, that even though she was a very young, spritely, fifty-nine year old, she would have to stay home!

The two groups were just finishing the exchange of information about themselves and the spiritual pathways they were walking when suddenly, I felt severe pain rip through my stomach and into my back; I gulped for air as I tried to control it. I shifted on my chair and stretched my spine in order to create more room for my internal organs. As the pain intensified, others around the table noticed that I was in obvious discomfort and suggested that I stood for a while; at that point I was not even sure that I would physically be able to stand. I tried to focus on my breathing in order to dissipate the pain.

Finally I gained the strength to stand. I rose gingerly, clinging onto the chair, as new bursts of pain ripped through my body. "It must be because we have been cramped in the mini-bus for so long. I do have a problem with my stomach and sitting too long is not good for me!" I told my new friends, in an attempt to excuse myself.

I racked my brain for an excuse to escape their prying eyes. Then slowly walked across the garden to the mini-bus to fetch the map of Southern France we had purchased, so that I could 'ask David's advice' on places of interest we could visit during our stay. As I leant into the mini-bus to retrieve the map, excruciating pain savaged me again. I could feel myself becoming frustrated as tears stung my eyes. Why, I questioned, was my life always such a battle between what my mind wanted to do and the limitations my body set?

The pain continued, it perplexed me somewhat and although I had made the excuse of travelling for a long time, I knew that was not really the case. The severity of it subsided and I ambled back across the lawn to the patio. Suddenly, it was back with vengeance, racking me with intense pain once more. I sat on the low wall that separated the patio from the rest of the garden, making it more of an extension to the living area of the chateau. I tried to appear calm and casual, whilst my mind was racing.

What on earth could be the pain and where had it come from? It was unlike anything I had experienced before and yet could be likened to labour pains. When the pain passed once more I returned to my seat at the table as quickly as I could. The others were engrossed in conversation as I pulled my chair in at the table. Sue, who was seated next to me, asked if I was alright. Now back in control, I smiled and nodded to assure my friend that everything was fine.

I then tried to re-engage myself in the conversation by asking Faye, David's wife, about the therapies she practiced. I showed particular interest in the treatment Faye called 'Journey Therapy'. As she explained the process, I experienced an upsurge of emotion, feelings of painful separation, almost a bereft feeling and I struggled to hold back the tears that were suddenly welling in my eyes. This time they were tears not caused by physical pain but by emotions: raw, painful emotions.

I swallowed hard to bypass the lump that had formed in my throat. Images began to flood into my mind as the emotions intensified. I knew and, Faye knew, what was happening.

"You are ready for a Journey." Faye stated.

There was no need for me to answer – I knew that in this lifetime I really had to address a big issue – one that had manifested in a negative form in each incarnation I had revisited. This was an issue between the vile man who had sexually abused me in this lifetime and myself. Faye had been made aware of the presence of an area that required addressing urgently by my reaction and had offered her assistance in that simple statement.

Fear filled me as I realized that this could be the day! One that might put an end to the thousands of years of pain and suffering - the end of all the agony and suffering from this lifetime too! Pain had dogged my adult life, starting when I was sixteen years of age. Coincidentally it was at the same time as I had suddenly started having flashbacks to what I instinctively knew was a past life. I recall: -

"...It is dry and dusty; the hot desert air is burning my nostrils as I breathe heavily. The sandy particles floating in the air are stinging my eyes making it difficult to keep them open. I am aware of my heart beating rapidly as I crouch in a state of alertness, beside an upturned wagon. I am crouching there with my wife, my son and other members of my scantily clad, Red Indian tribe. I am trying to shield them, to hide them.

We are encircled by American soldiers on horseback. I can hear the thunderous sound of hooves, of what must be fifty soldiers on horseback galloping round and around us. I can see the dust rising from the ground as the horses continue to gallop round and round, I can hear what I now am able to identify as gunfire…as the soldiers fire their ammunition wildly into the air. They appear excited and enthusiastic and are shouting to each other using a language that I have no understanding of.

As I crouch in hiding, along with fear, I feel bewilderment; this is my first experience of the white man. Others had told me they were to be feared but I had no conception of how powerful they were. I had dismissed the warnings of other tribesmen and now here I was, an Indian Brave, crouched in fear, hiding from the intrepid white man.

Then the horror really starts… the soldiers begin shooting at my tribesmen, randomly firing at men, women and children. Frantic to save my offspring, I helplessly watch as women run from cover with babes in arms, dropping one by one to their knees as the bullets speed through them. Children scream, men attempt to take control of the situation, aim their bows and arrows in vain and fruitlessly lunge with their spears.

I remain hidden for the moment, crouching with my little family. Sweat prickles on my skin, fear pulses through my veins and confusion lies in my heavy heart. Then amongst the mayhem a soldier spots us and dismounts; he steps forwards towards our hiding place. Then he calmly and purposefully takes his gun, aims it and shoots my wife dead. He then instantly, with a smile upon his face turns the gun upon my poor young son who still is clinging to the arm of his dead mother. My son looks at me begging for me to stop what is happening and make the soldiers go away. The soldier seems to enjoy what he is doing, to be getting some sadistic pleasure from seeing the desperation in my eyes, as across the language barrier, I plead for my son to be spared… I remain crouching, stationary, paralyzed, powerless… As the gun discharges its tiny brass bullet, I cannot attempt to explain the horror that I experience as I witness the slaughter of my beloved son.

Then the callous, cold blooded murderer, meaningfully turns the gun towards me; as time stands still, I know! I know what is about to happen, I know that he is about to end my life... My heart is already broken. After watching my wife and child take their last breaths in front of me, writhing in agony, I now welcome death... Then he shoots me. I feel relief as I experience the bullet rip through my flesh. The pain is as intense as the pain that had ripped through my heart, as I had knelt powerless and watched as the soldier had executed my family just minutes before. Yet with the bullet lodged inside my strong muscular body, pain exploding across my abdomen – I don't die...

The strongest of human instincts ironically takes over and I battle to remain conscious. When the soldier realises that I am not going to submit to the inevitable and simply die, he sneers at me. Then as I am knelt before him, like a slave before his master, I am racked with emotional and physical pain beyond which anyone could hope to comprehend. All glory of the brave man I once was had been stripped from me. I was now but a shadow of my former self, the lone feather I had worn with pride now splattered with blood, hung limply over my brow. The soldier shows me no mercy as he slowly and purposefully takes his bayonet and, with one effortless lunge thrusts it through my right side – I pray for death.

As I am about to perish - as I take my last breaths, I look into the eyes of my assailant and, in a flash of horror I instantly recognise that they are the same eyes that stared back at me so menacingly as a child. The eyes... the same eyes... They are the very same eyes as the one who abused me in this lifetime. Those unmistakable eyes. Ones I would never forget - the windows to an evil soul. A soul that had once killed me lifetimes ago had for some reason chosen to hurt me again in this life. The realization stung – the realization that this incarnation is not the first in which he has hurt me took me by surprise! It left me with one huge question – WHY?

It explained how around the same time as the flashbacks started, so too did an inexplicable pain in my right side, that led to numerous admissions to hospital with suspected appendicitis, only for me to be discharged with no diagnosis. Ill health had dogged me virtually all my life, but had worsened as the flashbacks continued.

Often out of the blue, I would see the same scene over and over again. I would be the Indian Brave, crouching behind the upturned wagon, hiding from the soldier. Each time he would kill me, my wife and my child. Each time I would experience the pain, the trauma, the horror. In a strange kind of way, I accepted the flashbacks, although I did occasionally have pleasant flashbacks. One such pleasing scene was of the Indian Tribe, to which I had belonged in that lifetime.

The scene always began with me looking through the eyes of the Indian Brave, whom I had once been. I am standing in front of the doorway to my tepee. The dwelling is made from animal skins and has a clay coloured zigzag pattern around it towards both the top and the bottom and a blueberry coloured zigzag around the middle. Standing about eight feet tall and about ten to fifteen feet in diameter, it is one of the largest homes in the settlement. A feeling of pride washes over me as I stand and survey the land.

The settlement is on the border of the woodlands and the plains and so my tribe benefited from being able to hunt buffalo on the Great Plains and seek shelter from the nearby trees in the heat of summer. While the men hunted for food, the women enjoyed farming the land and the open spaces, which also gave the children a sense of freedom not experienced in today's times.

In the scene I am always watching my son playing with the other children in the central area in front of the circle of dwellings. My wife is always walking towards me carrying what looks like a basket of berries on her shoulder and smiling. I experience a warmth and a rush of love when my wife smiles at me. We are very much in love. In the far left of the scene a young woman is talking to what I can only describe as a medicine man or a wise man of some kind; whilst sitting on low stools outside his tepee.

Approaching me from the left is a small group of young Indian Braves, about my age. One of them calls to me and waves; I feel that he is my closest friend. A group of men and women are seated on the floor to the right of the scene, just outside the circle of homes. They are conversing whilst taking it in turns to move meat around on a large fire made from sticks. The village is calm, everything seems in order and it is idyllic.

Without analysis and, without explanation, I automatically knew the very first time I was a part of this scene that the key characters in it were known to my in this lifetime or were destined to be. I immediately identified my mother as the Indian Brave's wife, the partner whom in that lifetime I had loved so implicitly. When I first experienced the flashbacks, I was not yet a mother and yet oddly I possessed maternal feelings towards the young boy, who many years later I identified as the soul of my son Alex. The Indian Brave who had been my best friend I now recognised as my brother in this lifetime and my father had once been the tribesman, whom we had all turned to for advice, assistance and guidance. The other character that I recognised many years later from that scene was the young girl, who was talking to the wise man. She was my niece Lauren.

As the years went by and I revisited the scene time and time again, I searched for evidence of other current family members such as Ian my husband and other nephews and nieces. Although I examined the faces of the men, women and children who presented themselves as the scene played out, I was never able to identify any other people that are with me in this lifetime.

Over the next twenty or so years, flashbacks occurred of other lifetimes and other encounters with the same soul who had stared at me through the eyes the soldier; who had ended my idyllic Indian lifetime. They were the same eyes that had stared so hard, so evilly at me during the abuse I endured when I was only fourteen. In each flashback it was apparent to me that it had been the same evil eyes that had stared back at me in each lifetime, as he hurt me again and again and again.

Following the abuse, I had been referred to three different counsellors, only to emerge even more distraught and confused. Eventually I even enrolled on a Counselling Course in an attempt to learn more about how one copes with trauma, in order to help myself to move on from the experiences I had endured during this lifetime. I thought that by understanding the mind, I would find a way to cope.

As nothing seemed to help, I eventually felt that I had managed to place the whole sordid business in a box somewhere within my mind and keep it secure most of the time. I believed that I was finally 'over the abuse,' however it obviously still affected me.

No matter how hard I tried to ignore it, inside, I knew that there was something bigger, something deeper going on that needed addressing. Maybe Faye would be able to offer a means of solving the whole issue. Maybe this 'Journey Therapy' whatever it was, would get to the core, find the beginning of the destructive relationship I had had with 'that man' through the eons of time. Each story needs a beginning, middle and an ending... and so having lived through the middle, wanting desperately to find an end, it seemed that the only way was to somehow discover the beginning. Maybe Faye could offer me the chance to recover the beginning. "You are ready for a journey!" Faye repeated. I nodded.

No more was said. The conversation changed and the physical pain I had experienced, mysteriously disappeared. The group finished the food and wine and adjourned to the music room, where David shared with us his latest piano composition, prior to leading a group meditation. I was then supposed to give a demonstration of trance, having worked as a trance medium for over a decade. Unfortunately, the emotions that were hanging heavily in my heart made it impossible for me to relax enough for the blending process to take place.

As I apologised, Faye silently held out her hand.

Chapter Two

To Hell and Back

"Come on then," Faye said, "It's time we were off!"

For an instant I faltered, Faye seemed nice, she seemed genuine, but hadn't they all? Instantly, memories of the extensive search that I had made for a cure flooded my mind. I had spent considerable time and money seeking the elusive panacea to my physical pain.

I had suffered ill health most of my life, but since having my son almost thirteen years before, it had worsened. In actual fact, I thought to myself, the condition actually deteriorated not after giving birth, but when, six months later my maternity leave had come to an end and I had been given a date to return to work. Not that I was work-shy - in fact the reverse. I had always worked very hard and been keen to pay my own way in life. As a young child I was always offering to do little jobs for people to earn a few extra pennies. Then as soon as I was old enough, I took on a paper round and as age permitted, I had worked in a shop after school and cleaned house for an elderly lady on Saturdays.

On leaving school I was lucky enough to secure the job of my dreams in a laboratory. My employers generously sponsored my education and I eagerly made the journey each week to London, where I studied to be a microbiologist. It had been hard being a teenager, working twenty-three hours a week, attending college and studying, but I had been determined to succeed, and succeed I did!

The thought of being separated from my tiny son five days a week had been too much to bear. As the date to return to work had approached, I became more and more ill until my doctor advised that I should inform my employers that I was unfit to resume my duties. Instead of disappointment or worry with regard to the financial implications of my predicament – a huge wave of relief swept through my mind and body. I was able to stay with my son and would not have to tear myself away each morning.

Could it be, I contemplated, as I stood up to follow Faye that my mind was in control of my body to the extent that it was able to physically manifest pain within my body? On some level, had my mind realized that I must be kept in a state of ill health, so as not to suffer the pain of separation from my child?

Whatever the cause, my health had deteriorated quickly until I had been unable to even lift Alex. I was unable to bathe and change him. Yet to all intents and purpose I, his mother, had been there for him. I had breast fed him, cuddled him, loved him and we had been separated only by sleep.

By the time Alex had reached his first birthday, I had been diagnosed with candidiasis (an overgrowth of the fungus Candida within the digestive tract). As a result I had developed numerous food allergies and was taking high doses of medication to control the pains I was experiencing in my muscles and joints.

As Alex approached his second birthday, my health had deteriorated even further. I had developed cysts on my ovaries and the once intermittent pain in my right side had become permanent. As my parents tended to Alex and I whilst my husband worked, they could not help but despair as they watched the sparkle fade daily from their daughter's eyes.

"I feel like I am dying, mum," I said one day, "I feel like I am being poisoned and I am doing to die!"

Annie and Alan had tried to boost my morale, assuring me that things would get better; nevertheless they had lain awake at night worrying about what the future would hold as I had grown worse and worse. Finally, I was admitted to hospital for an operation to remove an ovary, fallopian tube and appendix. Upon analysis it was discovered that the appendix had tiny perforations, which had allowed faecal matter to leak into my abdominal cavity. I was in fact being slowly poisoned and, without the operation, the surgeon had estimated, I would have been dead within six months.

After the operation, my body had taken time to heal, having been weakened for such a long time. Just as I had begun to improve, a cyst had erupted on the other ovary causing more agony. I had desperately hoped that after my first major operation I would recover, be a proper mum and go on to extend my family. Alex was a blessing – I had always known that. Before his birth I had been told that due to an earlier diagnosis of endometriosis, I would be unable to have children; but the yearning for more children had been strong. The second cyst would rip away any dreams I had had of another child and as the cyst grew to the size of a grapefruit and the pain had become unbearable, it became evident another operation had to be performed. Again, following the operation, a long period of convalescence was necessary.

After the trauma of the operation became a distant memory it was obvious that I was far from well. My general practitioner diagnosed ME (later to discover that was a misdiagnosis and that I actually had an auto immune disease instead). I quickly found that my life was governed by the overwhelming urge to sleep and the list of symptoms grew. Depression; that had reared its ugly head time and time again re-emerged but this time it had gained momentum. This time I could not fight it. It made me realize that I was worthless and had no place on the earth. It had tricked me into believing that I had no choice but to escape the cruelness of life in search of a better afterlife. I then began planning. I had hidden tablets that I was supposed to have taken; I had written letters to my loved ones and I had even prayed for forgiveness.

On that fateful winter's night, I had calmly said good-bye to my husband as he went to work his nightshift. I had phoned my parents and then I had gone into the bedroom where Alex had been innocently sleeping. I had climbed onto his bed, laid my frail body next to his and lifted his sleeping arm wrapping it around my neck. This was to have been our last cuddle. I had then kissed his cheek before leaving the room. In the safety of my own room, I had tipped the tablets into my open palm and opened my mouth. The demon that had eaten away at me, consuming my will to live had whispered in my ear,

"You are worthless, you can't do anything, and you're no good to anyone. They are all better off without you - you are a burden to them all!"

Suddenly, just as I had raised my hand to my mouth and curled my lips around the pills, something from the core of my being had screamed, "NO! NO! NO!"

The moment had been lost, my strength had dispersed, and I had become weak again. Tears of frustration and relief had cascaded from my eyes until I had collapsed on my bed exhausted.

My soul had beaten the demon on that occasion but many battles followed. Between struggles I knew that the demon was merely biding its time.

Years passed with numerous operations and visits to hospitals filling every one. Each specialist and doctor had conducted their own tests and given advice, much of it conflicting. Hospital visits had been inter-dispersed with treatments from complementary therapists. Over the years I had received just about every complementary therapy listed. Each had promised hope of a cure or at least improvement. Each therapist had seemed nice; each had seemed genuine – just like Faye. BUT, I had thought, how long could I go on and on actively searching for 'The Magic Cure'?

Over the years as my health continued on its roller coaster, in order to help both myself and other people who were suffering, I trained as both a Spiritual Healer and Reiki Healer. I took a counselling course, trained in the art of meditation and began to teach it too. The new skills I had gained did help, along with the numerous self-development books that I read. Yet I still failed to realize that I was seeking outwardly what was inside me. I failed to understand how, along with my strong mind, I had the power to find my own peace. During the healing courses I had learnt that healing merely offers the patients the time and space in which to heal themselves – sadly, I had never truly understood what it meant to heal oneself.

Lindsay was part of an organization called Herbalife and had told her close friend and colleague, Jane Clark about my problems. And Jane had, like so many before her, promised to help. Jane however was different. She offered to sponsor me for a year during which time she would supply me with minerals, vitamins, proteins and basically all the body's nutritional requirements free, whilst I followed a strict anti-candida diet. I willingly, though a little apprehensively, had agreed to the programme. Jane then had enlisted the support of Dr. Jamie McManus (based in America) and the programme had been set.

A year on, I had felt much much better. Jane's Herbalife programme had restored the natural chemical levels within my body and my symptoms had begun to subside a little. Gradually, I noticed that I was able to cope with more of life's demands and I tried to keep to the prescribed intake of vitamins and minerals etc. When the trip to France had been arranged, I had felt quite optimistic with regards my health, but as the date drew closer I had begun to feel unwell again.

So the holiday in France turned out to be like any other trip for me - a gamble. I never knew how well I was going to be. As the date of departure for France had approached, I had been increasingly more concerned. I tried to play down the extent of my condition to the other members of the group but the truth was that I needed to sleep for one to two hours each afternoon, was limited in my ability to walk due to the pains in my knees (caused by the recently diagnosed autoimmune diseases of Lupus and Sjogrens

Syndrome), I suffered constant headaches and, generally felt great malady.

Little had I known that the illness had probably worsened as a last ditch attempt for the demons within my mind, to stop me from finding Faye. The year-long work which Jane had been doing with me had prepared and supported my physical body, nourishing it and rebalancing it, in order for me to be strong enough to undergo what was to happen to my mind, once I met Faye.

It had all been a part of the plan, the bigger picture. Some force had been guiding me to meet the right people at the right time. It was time now to move on and so I had finally met Faye. Strangely the group had originally decided to holiday that year on the South West Coast of Turkey, where Sue had a holiday home in a small village nestling in the mountains between the town of Fethiye and the world famous resort of Olu Deniz. The preparations for the trip had commenced but as time went on an outbreak of bird-flu in Asia began to worry Rusty, who nervously outlined the effects of the disease to the others. As some members of the group were apprehensive, we all finally agreed to take a break nearer home and so the house in Laroque was located and suddenly as a group we found ourselves in France! Strangely enough once we had secured the rental and booked flights to Perpignan the spread of bird-flu ceased and it never reached Turkey!

Faye saw me falter and smiled warmly at me. The others in the room turned to look at me. They all seemed to be saying,

"Go for it!" to me.

What had I got to lose, I thought, as Faye gestured that I should follow her?...

Chapter Three

Preparing For The Journey

"Come on then," Faye said, "It's time we were off!"

Finally, powerless to resist, I followed Faye down the cool stone steps and into the guest annex where I settled myself into the red, upholstered, armchair as instructed. My body language said that I was relaxed but inside my mind a discussion was taking place. One aspect of myself was saying that I should keep myself in check, not allow my mind to listen to this nonsense, not to follow the journey process, whatever it might be. The other aspect was saying that I should trust Faye and grasp the help she was offering, follow the process and resolve my emotional issues once and for all.

Faye placed some clean soft tissues on my knee and explained that all that was asked of me was that I relax and put my trust in her. Trust surprisingly won the battle within my mind. I decided, even though Faye had said I didn't need to say anything at all, to share with her the brief outline of what had happened to me in this lifetime, by simply stating that I had been abused by my best friend's step-father when I was fourteen.

I then went on to explain the numerous flashbacks I had had since the age of sixteen. Incidentally this was around the time I had had to face my abuser in court. Court was very different back then. In those days, whatever the age of the victim, it meant standing in the witness box whilst the 'accused' sat across the courtroom from you, next to his/her defence councillors. There was no protective shield; no video-cam set up in another room, no social worker or liaison officer ensuring that the victim was OK. I, like many young girls of my time, had had to endure the ordeal of not only being in the same room as my abuser again, but also literally facing him whilst being intimately questioned by his lawyers – thank God for the advancement of the video link.

I remember vividly my time in the courtroom and, of being made to feel I was the perpetrator and of being belittled by his lawyer. I remember my abuser staring at me through the eyes that had tormented me throughout time, across the courtroom only feet from where I stood alone.

As I sat in the silent room with Faye, I experienced an upsurge of the emotions of those days spent in the court room decades ago. I recalled the fear of having to face HIM, of having to be in the same room as HIM again. I recalled the apprehension and vulnerability of standing alone in the witness box and the embarrassment of a young innocent teenage girl being ordered, by law, to explain in minute detail in front of my father and a room full of strangers, both male and female, exactly what he had done to me. It was the worst possible position to place any child in, let alone a shy, young teenager. And while I stood there, I knew how helpless and distraught my parents were, knowing their beloved daughter had to suffer in this way.

In the worst moments during the trial, as I was asked to describe specific details that seemed so irrelevant to me, such as which hand did he use initially to abuse me, I felt the tears fighting to escape as I was emotionally transported into the room in which I had found myself alone with him on that fateful day. Of course I remembered such details, but I didn't wish to share them with the room full of strangers, who were staring at me, searching for evidence that my words were a true account of what had occurred. For a moment I faltered, should I just back down and give up, save my parents and myself any more pain. It would be so easy to give up. As I looked across the courtroom at his smug expression, I suddenly was filled with strength. I thought,

"He has made me cry too often in the past and he is not going to see me doing it again now!"

So as my face flushed I took a deep breath. Standing to my full height, of five feet eight and a half inches, I looked over my shoulder to where my father was sitting. Court officials had seated him behind me and I was glad of the additional confidence he offered. As I looked to him now for confirmation that I was doing the right thing he smiled back at me offering me the 'thumbs up' signal. Without further hesitation I began to tell the sordid story with renewed vigour.

I explained to Faye how I had regressed myself previously using a technique called Merkaba Meditation, to a lifetime where I had lived in Edwardian Scotland. During that lifetime, I had been married to an eminent doctor. From the flashbacks I had experienced, I had deduced that we had a good standard of living and lived in a big house with an impressive entrance hall, I recalled. I had been well-dressed and obviously lived a privileged life. However, the price of my good standard of living was that I had to be seen to publicly support my husband.

The scene that came to me was always the same; it began when I, as the wife of the doctor, was sitting at the edge of a stage. The stage was not raised, as one would expect but was sunken so that the stalls were raised in a semi-circle around it. A large chiseled grey stone box-like structure of about seven-foot long by three foot wide and four feet high was the focal point and took centre stage. On the box like structure lay a man, naked except for a thin piece of cloth covering his groin area.

The man had unkempt, thick, ginger hair and bushy eye-brows. Thick course hairs of the same colour protruded from his short muscular legs and his arms as well as his chest. He was clean shaven and yet a faint impression of a beard could be seen on closer examination. The man looked about forty and in good health, if not a little dirty, except for a section of hair at the back of his head that was matted with fresh blood and a newly formed bruise on his forehead. The man lay motionless, his feet ending about a foot from the edge of the box like structure and his head nearing the top. To the man's right hand side, stood my husband, the doctor and, to the man's left hand side stood a young man wearing a white coat.

As I looked up I could see that many young male students and other medical doctors were in the theatre stalls watching my husband. As he spoke it was obvious that they were in awe of him. Any wife would have been proud of her husband being honoured by so many and yet as I sat at the edge of the stage I was consumed by an awful feeling of dread. I despised my husband, hated him and the work that he did. And yet I sat there smiling obediently as my husband cut open the cadaver and exposed his innards. As he expertly located the poor man's various organs and removed them from his body, I mutely sat there. As he described the functions of each, I sat in silence. As he finally, to a rapturous applause, threw a sheet over the man and cast him aside as one would a plate once the meal had been consumed, I quietly remained seated.

Then, as that scene faded, I suddenly found myself back in the big house. I was standing in the impressive hall looking forward, behind me is a huge wooden black door that was about five feet wide, and glazed with nine tiny coloured panes, arranged in groups of three. Under my feet were highly polished, geometric design, black and white floor tiles: to the left of me, in the spacious hallway, stood a reception table with a silver platter placed upon it and, beside it a plain, coat, hat and umbrella stand of square design.

As I hung my full length black velvet coat, there was a knock on the scullery door. I peered down the long reception hall and into the kitchen in hope that I would be able to see into the scullery in order to determine who was at the door. On noticing my inquisitiveness, my husband shouted at me telling me to go away so he could deal with his guest. He stood in the hallway glaring at me, ordering me to go to my room like a disobedient child and in that moment, as he stared; I recognised that his eyes were the same evil eyes, the same eyes that have haunted me throughout time.

I turned to obediently climb the ornate staircase and satisfied of my retreat my husband turned his attention back to the gentle rapping on the scullery door. I stopped halfway up the stairs. Through the reflection in the oversized mahogany hall mirror, that was perfectly positioned to allow me a view of the scullery door, I caught a glimpse of our house guest. It was a sinister looking man with pointed features. He was shabbily attired in a long black coat and top hat. He was dressed as though he had not a penny to his name and yet wished to retain a level of status within society. He appeared to me to be the type of obnoxious person whom one would instantly take a dislike to, as did I.

As the wife, I listened to the whispering voices. I felt bile rise in my throat as the all too familiar sick feeling washed over me. Instantly I knew that the two men huddled together in my scullery were making arrangements for the next delivery of cadavers. They were plotting their next murders. I listened in horrified silence as my husband placed his order. He wanted men, women and children, freshly killed, with no obvious signs of their fate. He wanted healthy people, people who had lives, who had families and homes – he wanted fresh meat! As my husband made his order he spoke of the victims as if they were inanimate objects, creatures without feelings, without the right to live. I deduced that the 'sinister looking man' was visiting the slums of Edinburgh and taking the lives of those who had been ordered by the eminent doctor for the purpose of his next theatre lecture.

The doctor and his 'friend', I realized, were murdering innocent men, women and children to create the cadavers. They were not grave robbing, which was common at that time, but actually murdering to create the apparatus required! In that lifetime I had again been afraid of him, had hated the things that he did, hated who he was and yet once again he had held the power to control my life.

I was powerless, unable to leave him, for there would have been no provision for a woman such as myself, without a husband, without a job or a family to rely upon. There was no question of divorce in those days; therefore I was totally dependent upon him. I had to put up with my existence knowing that if I spoke out there was little chance that I would be believed and even if I was, he would immediately have me executed. I had lived in fear of him finding out that I actually knew what my husband and his accomplice were responsible for and yet, secretly hoped that someone knew and would speak up.

Once again in that lifetime, HE had power over me. The same eyes, the same soul had exuded power over me, instilled fear into me... controlled me... ruined my life!!!

One of the other lives I had visited during my Merkaba meditations was one in which I was a young Egyptian boy of about eight years old. He had been sent to be an apprentice to a well-respected apothecary.

As I viewed the scene, I was aware of six stone steps leading down into a domed subterranean laboratory. As I took in my surroundings I saw there were shelves carved out of stone that were lined with neatly labelled bottles, each containing either liquid or small crystal flakes in an array of colours. Running through the centre of the room was a stone bench covered with a variety of glass vessels along with sets of pestles and mortars in ever decreasing sizes. A mixture of what appeared to be finely chopped grasses lay next to the largest bowl with two or three glass jars containing pink coloured liquid inches away.

The floor was of uneven stone, the same grey colour as the walls, bench and ceiling and in the corner stood a huge water container made of wood, which currently contained only a small amount of water.

As I stood there drinking in the scene my arms, those of the tiny eight year old boy, became heavy and I was instantly aware that I had in each hand a bucket filled with water. Perplexed, I wondered what to do with the overflowing water, when suddenly an authoritative voice demanded to know why it had taken 'the young boy – me in that lifetime' so long to get the water! As the voice echoed around the room I raised my head to see from whom it came. In that moment I instantly recognised his eyes. The eyes were the same eyes that had seemingly wreaked havoc as they followed me from lifetime to lifetime.

As the scene danced forward in time I was aware that the young boy had fetched and carried and watched his guardian until he was old enough to learn the trade himself. It was at that point that he discovered that his master was not always making the prescriptions, as he should be. He discovered that all the years he had known him, he had been playing 'god' with the cures. I realized that instead of being the well respected professional that others assumed he was, the apothecary was actually a wicked man abusing his power. I understood that he wanted the young apprentice (me) to follow his example, to play 'god' by harming those who crossed him in any way. It had been when I had refused; that young man's – (my) life was made very difficult until ultimately I had no choice but to comply.

The poor boy had no option - he was far from home, uncertain of how to return to his parents or if they were even still alive. He was trapped in what had become a living hell. The innocent boy could resist no longer and finally allowed himself to be turned into a bad man himself. There was nothing he could have done to prevent his fate, as the evil pharmacist wielded too much power over him. Eventually, the innocent young apprentice had turned to the darker side of life, and once he entered the dark side, there was no way back. Again in that lifetime it was the eyes that I had recognised during the regression! The eyes of the pharmacist were the same penetrating ones that had taunted me throughout history.

Faye suggested that we start the session at the point where I was transported during our discussion over the meal earlier. Instantly I recalled bewildered,

"...I suddenly felt loss and separation, distraught." The feelings that came flooding back along with Faye's calm voice transported me instantaneously back to the lifetime where the feelings originated, with great clarity, I began to relay what I was experiencing: -

"I am about eight, I am a boy and I live in Egypt."

As I focused on the small boy, I recognised him from previous flashbacks I had had. Those flashbacks had only ever been short and over the years had never expanded. It always began with me being a young boy. As the young boy I was aware that I was wearing crudely made, brown rope sandals and a simple, long white robe pulled in at the middle with a rope belt. In this scene I always felt happy, loved and carefree. Each time I had visited the scene I had felt the strong rough hand of my father holding onto my small soft one, guiding me along a road. The road was of uneven, blocks of rock that had become smooth over time, under the feet of those constantly travelling along it. As the scene played out, I happily walked along beside my olive-skinned father.

For many years I was not able to see the face of the man, who silently accompanied me and I was content in the company of the safe feeling that embraced me as we travelled together. One day I was surprised when, as we travelled the familiar road, I was able to raise my head far enough to make out the features of my father. To my astonishment it was the face of someone that I recognised. It was the face of a spirit that had appeared to me regularly throughout this lifetime. It was the face of the person that I called Abu. The insight I gained in that instant, explained to me why the spirit who had frequently accompanied me during difficult times in this lifetime, had taken such an interest in me. He had once been my father!

In the usual flashback, Abu and I continued our memorable walk passing numerous other people all similarly dressed. They nod and exchange pleasantries with each other as they pass us by. Periodically we stop to examine the contents of the various sized baskets that those we pass are carrying. I experienced the excitement that the little child does as he peers into the baskets to view their contents.

In-between the distractions I ambled along, curiously standing on tip-toes, trying to see over the grey, stone wall that edged the road. At certain places along the wall, there were small gaps, big enough for me to see through to the other side. On the other side of the wall was a steep incline that was dotted with clumps of coarse grasses and as I looked through the peep hole, I felt scared at the thought of the wall falling and the possibility of my rolling down the slope into unknown territory. I had never ventured beyond that grey stone wall that encircled the whole town and shivered at the thought of finding myself outside of this haven.

The walk continued, when unexpectedly I felt an excitement in the air. People began rushing towards a house on the corner of the road and Abu and I joined them. As we approached the house a crowd of about twenty or thirty people were gathered outside the entrance. I instinctively knew that those gathered were all my neighbours and I felt comfortable with each of them. The family, who lived in the house, had a visitor and it seemed that everyone was keen to meet him. I, as the small boy, drunk in the excitement and began to eagerly search the crowd for my mother so that she too could share in the anticipation of meeting the prestigious guest. I couldn't see my mother and began to panic. I loved my mother so much and hated being away from her... The scene always ended at this point, the point where I was standing with my father but franticly attempting to locate my mother. I was always unable to see the visitor or locate my mother and so always returned to the present with feelings of excitement and also of loss and separation.

"I am about eight, I am a boy and I live in Egypt." I relayed to Faye.

"I feel like a helpless child desperate to escape the future that has been chosen for me. My name is Hassat and I love my town, my life and my parents. I love my parents with all my heart and soul. They are kind, gentle people and they adore me too. Yet they have just told me that I have to leave them, that they will be taking me to another town, where I will be an apprentice to an apothecary. They have told me I will have a better life as a result. I feel panic, fear... I have never been out of our town. I don't know what an apothecary is but I know that separation is imminent and I feel bereft."

I became aware at that moment; that in the short excerpt from my life as Hassat, which I had frequently been privy to, that the visitor to the village had been the apothecary and the reason that I could not find my mother in the crowd was because she was inside the house talking to him.

Faye interrupted my thoughts as she sympathetically and simply stated "That's where we will start then!"

It had been obvious that I had already journeyed into the core of my being many times. From conversations we had had prior to entering the annex room, Faye knew that much of the preliminary work that would normally be undertaken during "Journey Therapy" had already taken place. I had studied hard – carried out much work upon myself and was already in touch with my soul. However, it had been obvious to Faye too that there was **one big issue** that I had not been able to work through alone. It was for that purpose that we had been brought together that day; of that fact we were both aware.

It seemed incredible to Faye that Carol's chance meeting with David several months earlier, in the UK had been enough to set up the barbeque that would ultimately lead to us working together this hot day in May. On examination, it seemed ridiculous - no-one in their right mind would spend four hours travelling each way to have a barbeque with a group of people whom none of them actually knew (with the exception of Annie, who had briefly met David on two occasions previously)! Who would travel a distance equal in time to travelling from London to Cardiff by car, just to have lunch with people they didn't actually know? In the same time it had taken us to drive to David's home we could have flown from the UK to Turkey, the Canary Isles or Moscow. It was also incredible to Faye that my soul had led me to France and more importantly to her, whilst at the same time my consciousness had been completely oblivious as to why.

Faye had explained to me that she considered me suitably in tune with my soul not to require the complete Journey therapy, which I understood. As she looked at me, sitting upright in the armchair, arms placed by my sides and hands relaxed in my lap, she could almost physically see the issue I was holding onto with her physical eyes. She likened me to a pressure cooker about to blow! It was usual for Faye to spend a great deal of time with her clients, identifying the central issue, and yet here was I sitting opposite her, virtually handing it to her on a plate.

I had an idea of what was about to happen, although it would have been impossible for me to have had a remote inkling of the enormity of what was coming next. A cleansing at soul level, an understanding of my thoughts, feelings, attitude, depression and personality would soon be mine. I was soon to discover how and why the complexities of my personality had developed. My understanding was to be a reward for my many years of hard work. I would soon hold the prize, the trophy, and the answers that had eluded me and complicated my whole life.

"Are you happy to start there?" Faye asked.

I nodded and immediately closed my eyes and began to breathe deeply; I relaxed my body using the same technique I employ during meditation, tuning into each part, commencing at my feet and working upwards to my crown. By choosing to work upwards in this way, as opposed to downwards, assists me to raise my consciousness. It aids me in lifting my vibration away from the physical realm and thus allows me to tune into the finer energies of the spiritual realms. The technique gives me the feeling that I have virtually put my body to sleep. Somehow I quietened my mind, managing to slow the thousands of thoughts swirling within it. I then focused myself upon Faye's voice and finally, as I lowered my head, Faye knew that I was ready to begin.

Faye then asked me to visualize and walk down a flight of stairs and told me that at the bottom I would find a doorway. I did as instructed and was, on reaching the door, told to open it and walk through. I pushed open the large, weighty, wooden door with big black hinges and a heavy, black circular handle.

Chapter Four

The Journey So Far!

The door opened into a room and there, stood Abu; he looked concerned and had obviously been awaiting my arrival. I felt comfortable with Abu. I had had a very close relationship with him for many years. My first memory of the tall, thick set, olive skinned, Arabic man was when I was about two and a half years old. It was mid-winter and I had been suffering, yet again, from a severe bout of bronchitis. Thick phlegm congealed in my throat, blocking my windpipe, which frequently left me gasping for air. My parents took it in turns to sit with me day and night ensuring I did not choke. It became routine for them to insert their fingers into my tiny throat and hook out the offending blockage. I clearly recall one of these occasions when my windpipe had been blocked and I had been gasping for air. The room 'went misty' and a kind looking man, dressed in white robes that touched the ground and tied at his waist with a rope, peered from under a white headdress through very dark eyes. He had stepped out of the mist and had held out his hand which I, as the weak, young toddler had taken, without question. I clearly remember the panic and fear subsiding at that point and a warm comfortable feeling enveloping me, as I unquestioningly, was led away into the mist. Although I have no recollection of where he took me, or what was through the mist, I knew that I had been happy and content with him there. I also recall him bringing me safely back, stepping out of the mist and as he gently let go of my hand, falling back into my bed and into myself.

From that day onward, the man whom I eventually came to know as Abu often came for me. I remember the twilight world fondly, when I could be with my special friend. I soon was able to recognise when Abu was drawing close and I also developed a unique method of calling him to me when I needed him. I remember sensing Abu close to me in times of need and feel that he has probably always walked by my side and always will! As I grew, I came to understand that Abu was in fact my spirit guide. The spirit who had for some reason decided to walk beside me throughout this lifetime, guiding me, helping me, supporting and comforting me.

Abu was not the only spirit visitor I had had as a young child. My grandfather had passed over when I was eighteen months old and I cannot remember a period when, as a child, I did not see and talk to him as well. As I grew I had frequent conversations with him while alone on my swing at the end of the garden. Yet not once as I was growing up, did I consider the fact that it was abnormal to disappear for hours on end with a man that no one else was able to see or that it was odd to talk to my 'dead' grandfather. I also had an 'invisible friend' with whom I would play with and talk to frequently.

By the time I was eleven, my clairvoyance and clairaudience (my ability to see and hear those in the spirit world) had developed further; but with no understanding of my 'gifts' and how I switched them on or more importantly how to switch them off, I found that they were trying to communicate with me most of the time. In the still of the night, when everyone else in the house slept, my sleep was continually disturbed. As a young girl I reported that things happened whenever I was alone and that I had become terrified of the disembodied spirits, whom I didn't know, who came to me for help in the dead of the night. A frequent night-time visitor was a young boy of about seventeen, by the name of John. He had blonde hair cut into an old fashioned style bob, piercing blue eyes and was wearing a sky blue coloured shirt. I vividly recall to this day everything about him. He would shake my bed until I awoke and then, standing beside my bed, he would extend his hand towards me and always make the same statement,

"I am so lonely, please be my friend!"

Having been brought up within the Church of England, been confirmed into the faith and attending a church school, I was confused; I could not understand what was happening and what I was experiencing. It became obvious to my parents that something was seriously wrong with me; I was jumpy, tired all of the time and hated being alone. I became gaunt and transparently white. At first my parents thought I was in need of psychiatric treatment until, at an appointment with my doctor, it was suggested that they requested the assistance of our vicar. They took his advice.

The Church of England vicar had been kind, following the correct procedures for exorcising and blessing a house, but after three visits and no change to the situation, he reluctantly pointed the family in the direction of the local Spiritualist Church. Annie nervously went to the church, taking a friend with her for moral support, to see if it would be appropriate to take her daughter there. She sought the advice of those who ran the church and was surprised to discover that many children were, in fact, like me. Having been reassured, she took me to the church. At once I felt as though I was where I was meant to be. It felt like I had come home – the people who attended the church understood, and what's more could explain the things that I had experienced throughout my life.

I enjoyed the services that the church held; they followed the same format that I was used to within the Church of England. There were prayers, hymns, readings and even a sermon (address). The only difference was that in place of communion, a guest medium would pass messages to friends and family in the congregation from loved ones who had passed on. On my first visit, a medium gave me a special message from my uncle who had recently died. Even though I had spoken with him myself and passed messages to my aunt on his behalf, I felt elated at the communication I received from him through an independent medium.

At each visit I took the opportunity to question the church leaders. I had an unquenchable thirst for knowledge and read many books on the subject. The stories I wrote in my schoolbooks all related to the subject of the afterlife and even though I often received low marks, probably due to my teachers distaste at, or possibly fear of, my choice of subject matter, my focus remained strong. I knew I was different, that I stood out from the crowd in this world but what was important to me, *was* the real world - the world where I had originated and the world to which I would return.

By the time I was sixteen I was sitting in a development circle where I learnt to meditate, to open and close the doorway to my mind through which the spirits were able to communicate with me. I learnt how to be in control of my 'gift' and very soon found that I intuitively knew far more than the group leader and often taught her a thing or two! When the circle leader herself passed into the higher realm, the group welcomed a new leader.

Robin had moved to the area recently and offered me a wealth of knowledge. He had answers to many of my, as yet, unanswered questions. He also taught me new methods to stretch my development and enhance my personal growth. Above all, he understood me. I was so keen to continue my spiritual and personal development that I continued attending meetings through my college days. Even, years later, when I was married and pregnant and supposed to be on bed-rest, I attended the meetings, taking part while lying on a therapy bed. When finally I had to give up the meetings due to my deteriorating health, I began writing inspired poems, many of which were printed in various magazines. The more I wrote, the more came into my mind, until I had a folder bursting with meaningful philosophical poetry.

An AGM at the church in 1996, brought a request from someone called Sharon (Maddie) to teach a group of beginners – people new to the church and in need of direction, as I had once been. I, now almost thirty years old, offered my services and so began another chapter of my story. I formed my first group – The Searchers. I took to teaching like a duck to water and my reputation spread. Soon I was teaching two, then three, four, five, then….nine groups. Students came from four counties, some travelling over two hours each way to attend the lessons. Seeing the need people had to learn the basics of the spiritual philosophy I had adopted, I designed a three-year course to educate students on a variety of subjects that would enhance both their spirituality and personal development.

I continued my own development.

At My Graduation (Ian, Alex, Me, Alan, Annie)

In conjunction with my teaching work, I studied counselling, spiritual healing and the Reiki system before taking a teacher training course so as to gain a teaching qualification that would allow me to take my courses to even more people. I completely changed my career, giving up science for good in favour of helping people find their way in life – all the time struggling with debilitating health problems myself. The more time I dedicated to teaching, the more help and direction I obtained in my own life. However, the help I received did not stretch to my own health problems.

As time progressed I spontaneously developed the gift of trance mediumship and found it easy to slip into 'the mist' with Abu, while others from the spirit realm used my voice to impart words of wisdom and deep philosophy. Although through my spiritual work, I came to know many spirit helpers, none could compete with the bond that I had with Abu – the strong love link we shared was far deeper than any love experienced on this earth. As time went by, I came to know that Abu meant father in Arabic and that he had actually been my father in a past life - the past life in which I had been Hassat. And so it came as no surprise to me that it was Abu who was waiting for me behind the heavy wooden door as I commenced my Journey...

Chapter Five

The Journey

Faye asked me to look around the room for someone; a spirit helper who would act as guide throughout this journey. I looked around the very large, grey, stone room that seemed to be lacking a ceiling. A large fire was eagerly burning through the cut branches that had been neatly placed to give it a wig-wam appearance. Then Abu stepped forward as if to take the role.

"Abu is here, he wants to be my guide, but I don't want him to be!" I responded almost crying, because although I loved him so deeply, for some reason I did not want him there. At that moment I felt confused. Why would I want to push my loyal friend – my trusted companion Abu away? I felt perplexed and yet had an inner knowing that it was not right for him to accompany me on this occasion.

"That's OK," replied Faye in a tone that melted away my fears and told me all was as it was supposed to be, "Ask for someone else to come forward. Abu can watch. Maybe he has something to learn here too".

As Faye completed the sentence, a woman immediately appeared. She was very pretty with long wavy jet black hair, but was dressed in a way that did not seem fitting to her. I couldn't help but notice that her choice of clothing did not seem to suit her. I felt that she should be dressed in the same style as Abu and yet she was wearing jeans!

After informing Faye that I was now equipped with a journey guide, Faye asked me to look to the centre of the room where there was a campfire. I had already seen the campfire and found it easy to relocate as I was instructed to sit beside it. As I did, so too did the lady, while Abu stood a little way behind us.

With everything in place, Faye then asked me to recall the scene that had presented itself earlier and asked me to invite little Hassat, the young child that had just been informed that he was to be sent away, to sit down beside me at the campfire.

Me at the campfire

As I complied, little Hassat swiftly entered the scene and immediately sat beside me. He pulled his white robe down so as to cover his sandals, manoeuvred the rope belt so that it hung from his waist at his left side. His head had no covering and as he placed his hands in his lap he looked up at me trustingly with his dark brown eyes wide open.

Hassat then explained how he felt that he was being sent away from his parents as a punishment for some wrong doing on his part. As he continued to explain his feelings, I experienced the emotions of Hassat and once again felt the intense sadness at the impending separation - the same feelings that I had experienced over the meal earlier in the day, I noted. Hassat gave an explanation of how he felt as though he had let himself down by not being a perfect son and thus, his punishment was to be sent away from those he loved. I knew that it was much worse than that, I knew that little Hassat was not only being sent away but was being sent to THE man. The man who would take away his innocence, the man who would control his actions, the man who would eventually turn him to the dark side!

I later related the feelings Hassat experienced with regard to being imperfect with the trait in my own personality of continually striving to be perfect. At home, at school, at college, at work, as a wife, as a homemaker, as a mother, in fact in every aspect the relentless desire to be perfect had been the driving force in my life. This desire had been sapping every ounce of my energy, consuming every waking moment. The house must be clean and tidy, in case someone should call and find something was out of place, was my logic. If that were to happen, I would not be perfect in their eyes and that would mean the worst possible fate.

I also recalled the anxiety that I had experienced at the thought of being separated from Alex, as the date for me to return to work after my maternity leave had drawn closer. The feelings I had experienced had gone beyond those of an overprotective parent. They had bridged time to reawaken the feelings of separation that I had experienced in the lifetime that I was Hassat. The feelings had been so intense that perhaps my mind had invoked the very illness that I had spent so much time and effort trying to cure.

Faye asked Hassat to invite his parents to the campfire so that he could ask them to explain to him the reasons for their actions – why they felt the need to send him away. Abu stepped forward and sat beside him. Then to My surprise, the lady wearing jeans looked up and I knew at once that this lady was the mother of Hassat. They hugged Hassat and told him how much he was loved and explained that they had had so little to offer him that they had made the heart rendering decision to look for an apprenticeship for him. They believed that if they could find an apprenticeship for their beloved son, then he would have the chance of a better life. A future!

The family sat together in silence, as Hassat searched both of his parent's hearts for the truth of their words. Hassat finally realized that the choices they had made for him were made with his best interest at heart. Finally he understood that the decision was made because his parents had truly believed that it would help him progress, offer him a better life and, that most importantly, it was not meant to be a punishment. I looked at my former parents and could see their distress at the assumptions Hassat had made.

Faye then asked Hassat to speak to his parents in order to discover their feelings with regard to the separation. As he turned to do so he spontaneously felt the pain of his parents at having to let him go; he felt the love of his mother and the grief she experienced at this sacrifice. No words were necessary. At that moment Hassat knew for sure he had been not just a good son but also one who had been adored by his parents. He knew that they had chosen to sacrifice the joy of bringing up their son themselves in the hope that he would have a better life than they could ever have offered him. The need to be perfect within me seemed to melt away instantaneously as I oversaw the dialogue between the family of yesteryear– I knew that the exhausting drive would no longer consume my energy and that I could just 'be' from now on!

****

Faye then asked me to look at a huge cinema screen that had appeared behind me, one on which the Lords of Karma would play a scene for me. Two Lords appeared, each dressed in a floor length, pale blue robe tied simply in the middle with a golden rope belt. Each had the ethereal features of an angelic nature and sported corn coloured, shoulder length hair. They stood about three metres (ten feet) apart and held up their hands as if supporting something heavy. As I continued to watch, I could see the screen and I waited...within seconds a scene played out that could have easily been an excerpt from "The Thieves of Baghdad".

As I looked more closely I could see one of the thieves was myself in a former incarnation. This was a lifetime that I had not yet visited, a lifetime that I had been unaware of up until now. As the scene played on, I saw myself as a thief, who was fighting with a sword. Faye asked me whom the fight was against. That was when I saw them again – those dark evil eyes, full of rage, full of anger, full of hatred.

"It's HIM!" I exclaimed, alarmed.

"What happens next?" Faye asked calmly, offering me the confidence to continue.

I continued to watch as the fight played out between the two thieves, one of whom was myself, in that lifetime and one of whom was HIM - the soul with the haunting eyes. The fight was taking place within a damp underground cavern. The huge grotto was about one hundred and fifty feet in diameter and the smooth rock ceiling hung eight feet above us. We were fighting on what appeared to be a pathway, which was lined on either side with gold coloured trinkets, jewelled adornments and a variety of luxurious drinking vessels. In front of the entrance to the cavern was a cloth bag, laden with items similar to those that lined the pathway. The cloth bag seemed to be the focus of the anger - the objective of the fight.

The other gang member was older than I, old enough to have been my father. He was very angry and I instinctively knew that this was no play fight, no ordinary test of strength or skill; I knew that this fight was real! As I fought on, I felt confused, as I experienced a loving adoration for my opponent mixed with a deep loathing. The fight continued, one thief lunging forward, the other jumping backwards.

The fight became more intense as I agilely flailing my sword, began chasing him backwards, making him stray from the pathway and forcing him to clumsily climb one of the heaps of treasure. I wanted to stop, to stop this fight and to embrace my opponent and yet it was obvious to me that should I do so HE would certainly overpower and kill me. I knew HE was merely awaiting an opportunity to end my life. On and on the fight went, love, hate and confusion mingled with blood and sweat as the razor sharp swords bit into our bare arms.

"What happens next?" Faye calmly repeated as I continued to relay what I was experiencing.

Time then seemed to skip to the end of the scene, and I watched in disbelief as I fearlessly plunged the sword into his torso.

"I've killed him!" I stated in a matter of fact tone.

"I killed him!" I repeated a little disturbed.

Faye then asked why the fight had broken out. I said that I had caught HIM trying to steal some of the treasure that belonged to the whole gang of thieves for himself and had questioned his integrity!

"How did you become a part of the group of thieves?" asked Faye.

I explained that I had been a male child living on the streets. As this child, I was hungry, thirsty and poorly dressed. I had had to beg for food and I recalled that people had kicked me out of the way. I had been a nuisance to them, nothing more – then THE man had come along and 'rescued' me (the boy child). He had fed and clothed me, taught me everything he knew – loved me as a son. The little child had soon been transformed from a street urchin to the highly acclaimed 'son' of the leader of a notorious Band of Thieves. The boy had grown to honour and love HIM. We lived together, worked together, played together, and over time there had grown a strong bond between us.

The bond had been jeopardized and then severed the day that I caught the leader of the gang stealing from HIS own people. Honour amongst thieves was the rule that we had all lived by. It was our culture, our life – the one thing – the one rule that bonded us together. I, as the young boy, knew I had a choice, as we stared at each other in shock. If I said nothing to the others I would be betraying everything I had come to believe in. I would be betraying my culture, my lifestyle, 'my family'. In a split second a decision was made, this man was no longer worthy of honour. Realizing that HIS 'son' had come to that conclusion, HE had instantly drawn a sword on me - his 'son'. Obviously if he overpowered his 'son' his honour and position within the Gang of Thieves would be secured, his dishonourable intentions would remain a secret, known only to himself.

The fight had commenced and both parties fought for their lives. Both were angry and vulnerable as swords clashed; both were hurt and shocked at the brutal ending of their relationship. As silver sparks flew, HE was overpowered. Anger flashed across his eyes and as the fatal blow was delivered, hatred raged inside him at the injustice of the situation. He could not understand how the child whom he had rescued, offered a life to and nurtured; had grown into the young man who was able to cast aside all that they had shared, and had slaughtered him in cold blood. Instead of honour HE had seen nothing but disgust in the eyes of his 'son' and in the final moments of that lifetime, he felt betrayed. As life seeped from him, hatred and anger consumed his every thought. He died with those vile emotions raging through his veins, replacing the life force energy.

He expired with anger at his loss of power and, full of hatred, baying for blood! HE died baying for blood, blood which he had taken in future incarnations. HE died baying for power, power which he had exercised over and over again throughout the eons of time.

How long, I thought, can this hatred, this power, this anger continue? How many more lifetimes can this manifest?

Faye broke into my thoughts "Ask HIM to come forward now as the leader of the Gang of Thieves"

Reluctantly I did as requested.

"Then," Faye continued "Ask him how HE came to join the gang."

I asked HIM to come forward and he did so with bowed head. As instructed, I then asked how he had come to lead the gang. Immediately I had posed the question, a scene not dissimilar to that which had played earlier, flashed across the giant-sized screen. I saw HIM as a child; HE was a street urchin, begging for food. As I continued to watch I observed that HE was rescued by the previous leader of the 'Gang of Thieves'. With a flash of realization I knew that he had been the same as me.

"Once he was the same as me!" I answered, surprised to hear my own voice again.

"Yes!" said Faye gently, "Once he was the same as you. Once he was young, vulnerable and unloved. Once he had no-one to love him!"

Then as I looked at the child further realization dawned - HE had never experienced love! Throughout the numerous incarnations we had shared, I had always experienced love and HE had never been that fortunate. Probably due to the opportunity he first gave me when I was that child on the streets, I could love. HE had given me the potential to love and to be loved; he had given me a gift that I had carried with me through the eons of time. As I continued to observe the screen I noted sadly that the previous leader of the gang of thieves had not been kind to HIM. I realized that HE had never been loved by him, only used. The only love HE had ever felt had been from his 'son' from the original incarnation of me, who had eventually turned on HIM and killed him. I had in that first lifetime that we shared together, ultimately betrayed the only love HE had ever experienced. For the first time ever I actually felt sorry for HIM. In that moment, I understood why through incarnation after incarnation HE had sought power through his position within society and had shunned love to hold that power, I understood now why HE was unable to understand the emotion of love! Maybe he was incapable of love; his soul had been damaged at its core while mine on the other hand had been saved, saved ultimately by HIM!

I felt myself soften as the new thoughts and feelings filtered through my consciousness. What about HIM, I thought? HE has not had the realization I have. HE is still angry with me and still wants to exercise power over me. HE still hates me for turning against him and killing him. His subconscious still clings to the images that occurred somewhere in a distant lifetime; through the veils of time. This needs to end – we *must* find a way; we both need closure and we both deserve an opportunity to move on, I contemplated.

"Tell him," Faye again broke into my thoughts, "Tell him that you understand why he did what he did, and tell him that it is time now for you both to move on."

I felt I was strong enough to carry out Faye's instructions. In a bizarre way nothing seemed important now – the tables had turned and it was now bizarrely about helping HIM. Abu had once tested my powers of forgiveness by showing me an image of HIM lying in the road after a traffic accident and had asked me:-

"Would you give HIM the kiss of life?"

At the time, the test was too much for me and I was thrown into turmoil. How could I put my lips onto HIS lips and breathe life into HIS body? How could Abu suggest that I do such a thing? ... Finally now I understood the message of Abu's test... HE was dying, just as a man on the roadside in need of the 'kiss of life' would be - HE was dying. HIS soul was shrivelling and it was up to me at this moment NOW to forgive HIM and thus grant HIM freedom within HIS soul. I knew that HE deserved to experience love and to live! Yet this was more intense than to place physical lips upon lips, it was about soul touching soul. Now I felt I actually wanted to free HIM - to breathe life into HIS soul.

...Silence in the therapy room...

"I've told HIM." I said, simply.

"Good," replied Faye "Now you can both start to heal. Wherever HE is now, whatever HE is doing now, HE will on some level be aware of the work that has been done. HE will change. HE will be different now. The ending is within reach for him too."

Relief swept through me on all levels of my being. It was as though my soul had given a huge sigh of release. It felt as though I had been fighting a battle for thousands of years that had just finished. The battle was over and we had all won, I realized triumphantly.

Faye gently coaxed my attention back to the campfire. Hassat was still sitting beside me, so too was the jean-clad lady and, of course, Abu. The big screen still hung in the air behind me and The Lords of Karma stood on either side of it.

Faye thanked the Lords for their assistance in the process and, as she did, they disappeared, taking the giant screen with them. Hassat looked up again at me with his dark eyes.

"Take Hassat onto your lap!" instructed Faye, "Squeeze him tightly, tell him that you love him and you will always look after him."

Tears cascaded from my eyes and a lump quickly formed in my throat. The words stuck - they seemed too big a commitment to make! Faye sat silently watching and waiting.

To say that I loved Hassat, to me seemed to be an outward acceptance that we were one and the same soul. That Hassat was perfect after all, would mean that I too was perfect! Yet to promise to look after him always meant that I would look after myself. My best interests were our best interests. It seemed too deep, way too big. I struggled, the tears that were continuing to fall, were now drizzling onto my forearms. Hassat then looked deeply into my eyes expectantly and trustingly, as a child looks to its mother. This child needs me to love him, I thought. This child - Hassat, I realized, is my inner child and I must accept him, embrace him and nurture him. Somehow, through the lump in my throat that seemed to be restricting my vocal chords I croaked,

"I...love...y.you...I ...I ...will always look after you!"

Hassat smiled and the warmth that came with his smile penetrated the centre of my being.

"I love you and I...I...I w...w...will always look after you." I repeated.

Then again, "I love you and I will always look after you!" I repeated, this time strongly and precisely.

Hassat knew too that it was over now... he got up and silently left the campfire. Abu stood up and stepped back. The jean-clad lady, the 'mother' of me and of Hassat stood up and smiled at me. I then noticed that the lady was crying. She too had spent eons of time waiting for me to understand that living with the barrenness of becoming a mother and then having no child to shower your love upon, had broken her heart and that pain, she had carried with her through time. Tears of compassion smudged my eyes as she embraced me. Abu stepped forward and he completed the scene. Immeasurable love bounced between the trio, and time stood still. We were outside of time and space; we were a family that had been separated by linear time. A family that had once been, a family that could now finally lay to rest old ghosts and individually move forward. Finally we were released from false assumptions that had been made thousands of years previously.

Time came for the embrace to end. Tears once again trickled down my cheeks, dampening my thin sun-top. Almost sobbing, we retracted again, each into our own space and lifetime. The lady showed her tear-stained face once more and Abu smiled through his familiar dark eyes, as wide as saucers, now brimming with unshed tears. We had reached across time and touched the souls of one another and the mixture of emotions that the experiences had invoked still hung in the air of the room in France.

The jean clad lady and Abu were duly thanked and the campfire faded.

I found that I now stood alone, facing the heavy wooden door. On one hand I wanted to rush back up the stairs to my life, to my current incarnation; but on the other, I wanted to stay in the room and consider what had happened. The choice was not mine to make as Faye gently guided me back up the stairs and allowed my conscious and sub-conscious minds to merge again.

Chapter Six

A Need To Be Alone

6

As I brought my consciousness back to the room I noticed that my arms were wet with tears and my cheeks prickled from the salty stream that had flowed down them. I dried my eyes, took a sip of water and stood up, unsure of how I felt or how I was supposed to feel. I leant forward and hugged Faye.

"Thank-you!" I exclaimed. It seemed insignificant but it was all that could be said.

It had been so simple, yet I had found the beginning and now it could end.

My eyes still red, my heart open and sore; I walked barefoot back through the château to find the others. The hot sun had disappeared and the clear sky showed off its millions of twinkling stars. The night was decidedly cooler than the day had been and I shivered as I rubbed my bare arms. I glanced at my wristwatch and then stared at it in disbelief! Three hours had elapsed! Three hours that felt like ten minutes. Guilt suddenly filled me, the others had been waiting for me all that time and the journey home was by no means short.

Stepping into the lounge, I noticed the wood fire crackling and laughter filling the room. The others were obviously having a good time and were not concerned about the hour. At that moment I felt as though all time was now. The trauma of each life seemed to merge into the here and now. It was difficult to distinguish between this life and those of the past. I felt that the experiences I had observed at the campfire had drawn me back to the past and then thrust me forwards into a new future. Someone gave me coffee and something sweet to eat. Lindsay moved to sit next to me and extended her hand to touch me in a manner as if to say – 'Are you OK? We are all with you!' The gesture was enough. Any more displays of support would have been too much at that moment.

We located our possessions, thanked everyone for their hospitality and then we left for the long journey back to Laroque. It would be 3am before we would be home and, I felt exhausted. I was still finding it difficult to accept that what had seemed like ten minutes had actually been three hours. I didn't want to discuss 'The Journey', didn't want to think about it at all. I just wanted to be quiet.

Me (left) and Faye after the Journey

* * * * * * *

The next morning the sun shone through the shutters of the house in Laroque and the members of The Searchers began to file through the bathrooms. I however, lay in bed listening to the chattering, giggling and clattering but did not feel ready to face the others. I wanted to stay in my room alone – I didn't feel sad, didn't feel happy but I didn't want to think or to communicate. I needed to be alone.

I was aware that the others must have been wondering about me. The schedule I had issued for the week stated that we should board the mini-bus at 12pm for that day's trip. Due to the late night, everyone was late getting up and there were things to take care of before we left, but I just could not bring myself to join the human race yet. Annie, with whom I was sharing a room and who is my mother in this lifetime, looked at me with concern. I could tell she was wondering if the therapy had made things worse. I knew that Annie would be recalling the negative outcomes that had resulted from the counselling sessions that had been supposed to have helped me in the past.

"It's OK mum," I reassured her, "I am fine - I just don't want to talk about it!"

I then tried to explain to Annie that it felt as though I needed healing to fill a hole that had been left within me. I explained how I felt by likening myself to an orange. If one segment, that had been rotten and been affecting the other segments, had been removed, I explained, it would leave a gap and make the orange peel saggy. I said I felt as though healing would plump up the remaining segments so as to stop the peel from sagging. Sue, who had entered the room now to check all was well, heard my analogy and offered to give me hands on healing, as she was both a Spiritual Healer and Reiki Practitioner. I felt that the time was not right – maybe it was part of the process to let the gap heal itself in its own time.

Maybe, I thought, the reason why people hang onto things that we should and could let go of, is fear of 'the gap'! It seems that we wrongly feel that keeping every experience that has affected us within our conscious mind, no matter how painful it may be, is preferable to letting it go and dealing with the space it leaves. It is scary and an unknown quantity – there is no one to tell one what to do with 'the gap'. I understood now that I had held onto the negativity because in some strange way it was more comfortable than letting go. I felt this morning like I had let go and was now freefalling. This was actually enjoyable and, even though I knew after the fall I would be safe and well and a much braver person, I was scared of what might be. It felt as if I had just bungee jumped off a very high bridge. The good healthy experiences would expand now that the rotten ones had been taken away, but they would have to do so in their own time. I knew that as they expanded, the cleanness at having cast aside the rotten experiences would fill me with pure joy, calm and freedom. In the meantime I should just freefall!

It was a strange day –

The Searchers made our way aboard the hired mini-bus, to the sleepy fishing village of Colliour, where we had planned a meditation on the beach. After the meditation the group split; some remained on the beach while others chose to wander around the village. I sat alone on the beach and updated the journal I was keeping for the members of the group who had been unable to join us in France. I then joined Annie and Elaine for a dip in the warm

Mediterranean Sea. Too soon it was time to return home. On the return journey we stopped to eat at a more commercial, tourist town. We wandered from one restaurant to another. If the menu suited some, it did not suit others. I felt impatient; I had no preference so long as we ate! The dilemma went on and on until I finally exclaimed –

"Well I am eating here!" before disappearing into a crepe bar.

Surprised and mute, the others all followed and found that the menu the crepe bar offered was in fact extensive and the food served, delicious.

It was agreed that shopping must be done before we returned home and so after the meal I took a list from every one of essential items and armed with the list and eager to escape, I went to grab a trolley while Elaine – my appointed assistant – finished her drink. Shopping was relatively easy and quickly completed. However, as the day wore on I had recognized that I was feeling more and more claustrophobic around the others and a desire to escape them was getting stronger. I didn't know where the feelings were coming from and tried to subdue them as best I could by keeping myself to myself as much as was possible within a group of eight women.

By the time the mini-bus pulled into Laroque, I could stand it no longer. I grabbed the arm of Anne, who was sitting next to me and told Lindsay to let us out of the bus so that we could go and order the bread for the morning. (It was the only reason I could think of to use).

Bewildered, Anne followed my lead.

"I just couldn't do it," I exclaimed, once free from the mini-bus.

"I just couldn't cope with them all flustering around, unpacking the mini-bus, unpacking the shopping... I couldn't trust myself not to blow a fuse. I thought I'd be better if I kept out of the way."

Anne led me to some newly set tables outside a bar and ordered coffee for us both. For a while we sat in a comfortable silence; I enjoyed the peace and knew that Anne did not expect anything from me. When I felt able to cope with the group again, we climbed the steep cobbled slope, past the quaint little houses and small Catholic Church with its single bell hanging within its own tower that summoned the villagers to services. Past the clock that chimed loudly each hour; the one that could be heard throughout the village acting as a constant reminder that time was marching onward; until we finally were back at the house. I didn't understand how I was feeling but knew that it was important that I responded to the emotions I was experiencing.

Church Bell in Laroque

Time out was addictive and, on returning, I realized that I was not yet ready to rejoin the group. I entered the house and stopped, taking in the hustle and bustle. The shopping was being unpacked, the dishwasher emptied. Washing was being retrieved from the washing line in the small garden and someone was making tea. Usually I thrived upon such activity, enjoyed being in the middle of it, directing proceedings but today I was wary of it -didn't know where I fitted in or what I should do. My eyes flashed from one to the other of my closest friends and I felt panic rising within me. An urge to escape welled within me and I asked Elaine to accompany me on a walk around the village. I was comfortable with one person at a time but not the thoughts and feelings of the whole group at once. As we neared the house I wanted just a little more time. As we climbed the hill and approached the church, I knew that the next corner would reveal our temporary home and I was still not ready.

Almost opposite the church was a restaurant/bar that the group had eaten in several times that week. I looked at Elaine; no words were necessary as she intuitively knew that I was not yet ready to face the rest of the group. As I suggested we sneak into the bar, Elaine said she thought that was a good idea and quickly we disappeared inside. I knew the others would be waiting for us by now to start work – but I didn't care! For once I didn't care! I sat at the bar and, brimming with newfound confidence, ordered two brandy and lemonades – in French! They were expensive but I didn't care, everyone was waiting – but I didn't care! It was as though for the first time in my life I was doing something because I wanted to and not because it was expected of me or what I should do – something for no one but myself…. We returned when I was ready and the evening's spiritual work went very, very well!

Chapter Seven

The Butterfly Emerged

The next day was different! Again the sun shone in through the shutters. I leapt out of bed! I had no pain, was not tired and felt different. Later I realized that I had not taken my usual painkilling tablets and had only taken one dose the day before – I had not needed them. Then I noticed that the pains and creaks in my knees had almost gone and I could walk further - I could run and skip, even my legs seemed now to be free. I saw that even the eczema on my ear had disappeared. I did not question, merely accepted the changes that were occurring within my physical body but more importantly I was also acutely aware of the changes that were occurring inside my mind.

Me on a Bike in Laroque

Today, instead of needing to remove myself from the group, I wanted to be with them, to be in the bosom of my friends. However, I had changed; instead of feeling the need to organize everyone and everything, I just let things happen - let them be! I did not want to be serious, to have any responsibility, to make any decisions - I just wanted to play and have fun, I was embracing my inner child. The schedule had given us the whole day off and when the suggestion came that we go for a drive around and stop in a bar

for some lunch, we all agreed it was a good idea.   The group
boarded the mini-bus once again.   After driving for some time, we
came upon a cluster of shops and bars set around a small harbour.
We sat outside the first bar that we came to and ordered jugs of
sangria.   With no food in our stomachs a light, heady feeling soon
enveloped us.   Before the food arrived, large blobs of rain
periodically splattered around. At first it was refreshing but as it
came faster we retreated inside.

Eight of The Searchers in France!

Apart from an elderly local man and his grandson, the bar was
deserted, which, when we focused upon the drab décor, came as no
surprise to us.   The bartender put on some music and I began to
dance.
   "Come on!" I urged, "Dance with me!"
The sangria and my newfound sense of fun had erased my
inhibitions and as the group looked on; I jumped onto a small stage
in the corner and attempted to mimic a belly-dancer's routine.
Before long the whole group had joined in by either dancing or
clapping along to the music. I felt so free – I was so happy that I
thought I would explode. It was as though I had been hiding in a
dark, dingy cupboard and someone had taken me out, polished me
and made me realize I no longer had to hide.

I felt so happy, so playful, and so free! Something big was going on. I was acting like a child! Usually if I had a little too much to drink, I kept myself in check, never wanting people to think badly of me, not wanting to let myself down, always keeping the façade of being in control. Never before had I truly cast aside my inhibitions and revealed my true self. I realized that day, that I had not been in touch with my true self for many years.

After a fantastic day, the group arrived back in Laroque. When the others wanted to sleep, I wanted to play. There was no off switch. Now that Faye had guided me to find the on switch, there was no going back. Everyone noticed; there was no escaping the practical jokes, the humour and the zest for life that now exuded from the real me. When it was too late to be up and the group members had retired, I could not contemplate sleep. I still wanted to play! I went from room to room entertaining each of my friends in turn and playing jokes on them. The practical jokes only stopped when I had succeeded in making everyone get up again! When we were all holding our stomachs from laughing and our jaws ached, I finally gave up and went to bed.

A few days later I wrote in my journal: -

'After THE Sunday in May 14 – 05 – 06:
Each day starts with a smile now because -
It now really is NO MATTER!' In other words it does not matter,
it has no matter – so it has no form. It is there but it has no solid
form within me. As its' solidity vanished, so too did the great
heaviness that sat in my heart. I did not even realize that such
heaviness was there until it had gone. I now feel as if I have lost
half my body weight- I feel light, free and playful. I want to laugh
and laugh. I want to play – for – now I feel like I am the child I
was supposed to be! The noise in my head, that I thought was in
everyone's head, has just gone... it is silent now, only the thoughts
I put there are there. My head is sunny. I feel shiny and new and I
never knew I was dusty and old. My soul is full of love now!
It was so simple and it was there waiting.'

I returned home at the end of the week a completely different person. My twelve-year-old son greeted me excitedly at the door. After I hugged him, he stepped back,

"You look funny mum!" he stated.

"I am in summer clothes, is that why?" I asked, as I took off the glittery new headband I had brought while away and shook free my long, sun-bleached hair.

"No!" He replied looking me up and down "I want my proper mum back!"

That evening my son viewed me with caution and although obviously pleased to see me home safely, was unsure of the vibes he was picking up from his mother. The next day during a phone conversation with Annie – his grandmother, Alex informed her that his mother was in some way different. He didn't know why but she was changed. From their conversation, Annie deduced that he was perplexed and a little unnerved by the changes within his mother that he was unable to pinpoint.

My husband could not understand my newfound energy as I happily washed and ironed in preparation for our family holiday a few days later. His parting words to me as I left for France had been: -

"Now, have fun, but don't wear yourself out and make yourself ill for our family holiday!"

As the ten family members gathered to await our mini-bus to the airport, they too couldn't help but notice something about me had changed. I sat in the front of the mini-bus with my sister-in-law and chatted non-stop. I wanted to try to explain what had happened to me in France. How I felt and how I wanted everyone to be freed as I had been. I didn't feel the need to be in control, not of myself nor of the rest of the party. I realised that it was now safe for me to step back and let things happen naturally.

Everyone couldn't help but notice the playful glint in my eye, the boundless energy and the enthusiasm I had found for life. My brother continually made comments to Annie with regard to my laid-back attitude. Everyone noticed that I was enjoying life. They struggled to put their fingers on just what was different about me, but they knew that something had changed me - changed me for the better. I did not spend my time tidying up and trying to organize everything – things just occurred in their own time and everyone was more relaxed as a result.

During the holiday my niece innocently started a sentence with...
"Auntie Wendy, now that you are better..."

...And that summed it up - I was better – my mind was better. Faye had cured me from the 'demons' that I had materialized. These were the 'demons' that were my own response to what HE had done to me when I was fourteen years old and the memories that the abuse had triggered. I had not realized before that I had allowed the 'demons' such control over my every thought and deed, in addition to control over my mind and actions. As the journey had taken place, the 'demons' had loosened their grip and had fallen away, revealing me to the world as my true self. For a few moments as the realization dawned, I was saddened at what I had lost, at what HE had robbed me of and, what I could have been. I felt sad as I saw for the first time the person that I had been and how others obviously perceived me. No wonder, I thought, I irritated people with my bossiness and controlling personality. I felt sad at the detrimental effect that the 'demons' had had upon relationships with my friends and family. As the sadness embraced me, I felt one remaining 'demon' grip me and I came to my senses once more.

"You may have controlled my life, made me become something that I am not but your reign is over – I have won, I am free!" I stated loudly to my reflection in the mirror and the 'demon' loosened its grip once more.

On returning home from the week's holiday in Mallorca with my family, I wrote in my journal: -

'If I had known that three hours with Faye could make me feel like this – I would have sought her assistance a quarter of a century ago! I can't put into words the gift that she has given to me and on behalf of not just myself but my family too, I thank her from the bottom of my heart.

I wish I could take everyone to see Faye, I recognize pain in the eyes of others and I want to tell them that there is a way of making it stop. A simple way that does not involve the pain of traditional methods of helping that one uses to deal with trauma.

I want to share my story so that others may be encouraged to find the beginning and thus end the pain and suffering.'

I placed the journal on the table beside me, and then sat back, in my armchair. The window was open and the fresh June air filled the room. The sunlight reflected off the large mirror hanging over the marble fireplace and created miniature rainbows around the room. I gave a contented sigh. Three weeks ago today, I thought, I was boarding a plane bound for Perpignan. Three weeks ago tomorrow, I met Faye... I let my mind drift back to the lazy hot afternoon and the four-hour journey – for a barbeque!

I smiled as I recalled The Searchers' inner knowing that 'those above' had set up something special. Something utterly incredible, I thought, getting up from the chair.

"Mum!" My son called, "Are we really all going out now?"

"Yes," I smiled, "I'm better now! I *am* better now."

My husband slipped his arm around my waist and kissed me tenderly – lots had been missing from my life and thanks to Faye it was all now back on track!

Chapter Eight

The Proof Of The Pudding

8

"The proof of the pudding is in the eating." I heard Annie say, as the healer/therapist she was talking to, declared that he was able to cure patients.

That was her motto. As a Spiritual Healer (now known as an Energy Healer) and Reiki Healer & Master, tutor and assessor, Annie often came across practitioners who, usually through ego, declared themselves to be 'the best' in their field.

"Do your healing work diligently. I will give you all the support you need and, when your patients are cured, then I will know you have a gift more outstanding than other healers." She told him.

Not that Annie was trying to put the healer down or hold him back, but she had seen the damage that could be done by false claims and egotistical therapists. What she was saying was, 'I will wait until you have success before I get too excited.'

After my treatment with Faye, I had felt different within two days. Huge transformations had taken place in me as a direct result of the changes that had taken place within my mind. Yet Annie remained unfaltering in her stance, repeating her familiar motto: -

"The proof of the pudding is in the eating!"

I knew that I was eating my pudding and enjoying it! I felt like I had been changed from the heavy metal plumbium to the inert gas of helium. I was definitely floating on air!

Whilst family and friends could not help but notice the dramatic changes within me, Annie couldn't help but hold her excitement in check. Not that she was being pessimistic – far from it. She had seen my hopes and dreams built up and dashed on numerous occasions in the past and merely wanted to ensure that this therapy was not to be just another broken promise.

As the days passed, Annie had observed that my attitude had remained at the improved level. I had more energy and had appeared so much happier. I had tackled tasks that I could not have attempted in the past. Annie was shocked when she called on me one Sunday afternoon to find me on my hands and knees having almost completed weeding my garden path.

"How are you feeling?" Annie asked in astonishment.

"My back's aching a bit now mum," I replied

I think I have found muscles that I haven't used for years! But" I continued, "I did have a strange experience while I was gardening –

I thought it would be fun to tackle the garden myself for once but after half an hour of weeding in-between the little crazy paving stones of the path, I began to get a bit bored. I looked back to see that I had only finished about ten feet! For a moment I sat and stared at the tiny piece I had completed and then the big piece I had yet to weed. What happened next was the strange bit..." I said, pausing to look at my mother.

"I heard a voice, mum, in my head - perhaps it was my mind, I don't know but what I heard was profound!"

"Go on then," said Annie curious.

I continued, "The voice said, - 'It is not how far you have to go that is of greatest importance but how far you have come'!"

The voice had certainly made me sit up and take note. I had then continued with the weeding, deep in thought, reflecting on how far I had come since meeting Faye. In no time at all I found that I had reached the end of the task I had set myself, just as my mother had arrived.

Mum and I

A few days later I had to make an hour's journey along the coast for an appointment, in Hythe. I had made the trip several times and was used to the scenery. The day was neither sunny nor particularly dull, in fact it was quite a nondescript day. As I drove around one of the many roundabouts steering traffic around the port of Dover, I was suddenly aware that the grass decorating the centre of the roundabout appeared to be in some way greener. I puzzled as to why that could be as I drove towards the next circle. I waited my turn and then joined the stream of traffic mindlessly circling the next huge roundabout and, as I did so, the beauty of the trees that furnished the centre of that concrete circle struck me. The pure beauty of the trees, their shape, their colour, their essence, actually brought tears to my eyes. With a jolt I realized that I needed to turn the wheel and pay attention to the road. I quickly shook my head and focused through the tears as I steered the car off at the next turning.

I switched on the radio to distract my thoughts from the strange occurrence, but due to the fact I was driving below the cliffs there was no reception and so my mind had nothing but the thoughts of the strange events to occupy me. In the blink of an eye I seemed to reach my destination, with no further peculiarities.

On returning home and opening my front door, I looked slowly around my house - how could I possibly have missed this before, I wondered?   How could I not have seen such brilliance before? Everything - carpets, curtains and décor was so much brighter than I remembered it being when I left; yet I had only been out for three hours! I struggled to understand what was happening to my eyes, blinking them, and then rubbing them before looking again. I had always had 20/20 vision and yet for no apparent reason as I stood in the hallway looking at my own home, everything appeared brighter, shinier and crisper - it was as though I was looking through different eyes and seeing things that I had missed before. For the next few days I examined everything I set eyes upon and concluded that somehow my eyes had changed or, at the least, the way I perceived what I saw had!

I discussed the strange phenomenon with The Searchers at our meeting the following Friday morning and the group concluded that the strange visual experiences could have something to do with the Journey Therapy.   Brandon Bays, who discovered the immense healing power of the Journey Therapy, states that when a trauma occurs, then a memory of it is held within certain cells of the physical body. That memory is referred to as a negative memory and as the cell that holds it dies and a new one replaces it the memories held within it are passed on. Therefore, the negative memory is regenerated and is known as a Phantom Memory Cell. It is possible for the phantom memory to regenerate again and again manifesting ultimately as a physical imperfection. It could easily be the case that cancerous tumours are created in this way. Brandon had successfully cured her own tumour, which was the size of a basketball, with no orthodox intervention, whatsoever. Brandon relied upon the power of her own mind to rid her body of the huge tumour. It seemed to The Searchers, that a negative memory must have also been held within my eyes and once released, new cells had been generated - my vision improved or rather the way in which I was able to see colours did.

"Why had I not realized that I had a problem with my eyes?" I wondered.

Then I recalled a trip to the ophthalmist with my son when he was about seven years old. The ophthalmist had asked my son if, when he was trying to read, the words moved – up and down – side to side – or all over the page. I had been perplexed by the question and even more so when Alex informed him that the words moved all over the page. The specialist went on to explain that he had discovered a problem with the tracking mechanism of Alex's eyes (which has since been successfully rectified) and that was why it appeared to Alex that the words were moving all over the page. On the journey home I had asked my son why he had not told me that he was having difficulty reading because of this, and his answer was simple and yet had astonished me.

"Well, mummy" he replied, "I thought that is what happened when everyone read!"

The profound words Alex had spoken then came back to me now. One often does not realize that there is a problem until it is pointed out.

From the dramatic response to "The Journey Therapy" it was clear to me that I had brought, from past lifetimes, negative memories that originated in Baghdad. Those memories had been regenerated lifetime after lifetime, until they were finally reactivated in this lifetime when I was aged fourteen; resulting in the negative traits in my personality that controlled my life until I met Faye. The pain which had commenced in my right side felt as if I was being stabbed with a sword, I had explained to doctors at the time. After numerous admissions to hospital, I was diagnosed, after undergoing a barium enema, as suffering from a Dysfunctional Illiocecal Valve. When in Hythe, I had visited Alison, a kinesiologist for the first time, who explained that the illiocecal valve was considered to be the seat of the emotions. The penny had dropped. It finally made sense to me the reason why, after the abuse, the pain in my side had manifested as a direct result of the emotional memory that was activated.

Now I had stumbled upon the method that would not only sever the regeneration pattern of negative cell memory but, my scientific brain realised, I could actually use the power of my own mind to reprogram cells. It would therefore be possible to create a body that was in possession of only positive memories and thus a healthier body would be created. I thought long and hard about my thesis and, as I did, my friend Sue, a fellow member of The Searchers Group, came to mind. I had known Sue for about twelve years and, when we first met she had luscious long hair and a wonderful figure. When she was paid compliments on her appearance she would respond by saying;

"Yes, well that is now, wait till I am forty, I'll be fat and frumpy!"

By the time she turned forty, Sue had started to put on weight. At first she thought it was due to her giving up smoking and then realized there was something seriously wrong with her. Finally she was diagnosed as suffering from an extremely under active thyroid, which took a year to medicate correctly. In the meantime she had gained a substantial amount of weight and had lost both her confidence and identity. She had become exactly what she had programmed herself to be! Fat and frumpy! She then struggled for many years to regain her figure and self-confidence.

If it is possible to reprogram one's cells in such a negative way, I thought, it must be possible to reprogram them in a positive manner.

I had only four months to go before my fortieth birthday and had already changed my thinking to make progress in reprogramming my cells and, as even the most durable cells only live for six weeks, reprogramming should be relatively easy, I concluded!

However, Brandon's Therapy was not merely about understanding oneself, it was about understanding that we are all connected intrinsically by the same thread. I had always understood that fact and had known that it is important to not only learn to understand ourselves and our fellow man but to take it further and to make an effort to understand the energies of nature from the biggest of mammals to the smallest of insects; from the tiniest seed to the tallest tree.

My belief was strengthened after reading 'Living in the Field' by Lynne McTaggart and attending one of her conferences. I also understood how learning to blend with the elements; the earth, the air, the water and even the fire, until finally one is able to glimpse the essence of The Divine, assisted in personal development and in understanding the world in which we live. I had, in fact, been working towards this goal for many years. I even produced a meditation CD that leads its students to a point where blending is possible. Those who used the CD have had profound experiences and found it had expanded their understanding of not only the world but of themselves too. Other cultures understand the importance of blending. The North American Indians for example, regularly practice the technique of blending with the element of fire through sitting in a sweat lodge naked and, enduring the unimaginable heat. Only when our bodies drip with perspiration and our lungs feel as though we are about to explode do we feel we have truly blended with the element of fire. The sweat lodge meditations are said to lead the student towards personal enlightenment. Buddhists also practice meditating with the intention of blending with the elements of earth, fire, air and water before meditating upon what we refer to as empty space. It seems that cultures throughout the world understand the importance of understanding energies and the power of the link that binds us all. The same link that binds us to the past and to the future!

Having an understanding of not only my spirit but also my soul helped me to understand The Divine. I had always struggled with the terms soul and spirit and, during my Spiritual Development classes, I had often been asked by my students to define them.

Mind, body, spirit and soul were words that were branded about often within the 'New Age' and esoteric philosophies and yet, to find a definition was extremely difficult, I had discovered. After my journey however, I felt that I had gained an insight as to what each was; my own conclusions are as follows: –

The body was easy, for it was quite obviously the matter; the part of one's being that had form, the part that was matter and the part that does matter during an incarnation upon the earth! The body is the casing, the overcoat – the vehicle for the spirit.

The mind is a little more complex in that no one actually knows where it is; at present, scientists believe it not to be contained within the body. It has no solid form and is unseen to the human eye. The mind is individually connected to a particular body and is where thoughts, feelings and emotions are held.

The spirit, however, is the individual personality essence of a single incarnation. It is connected to the physical body while it is alive and then exists independently after physical death, whilst keeping all its attributes. It has no solid form but can sometimes be seen by those who have developed the art of clairvoyance.

The soul however, is the collective energy that contains The Creators' essence and the energy essence of the spirit of every incarnation it has experienced. The soul is the person that one was in each lifetime. Each spirit, experiences an incarnation; therefore many incarnations are experienced by a single soul. I, Wendy, Hassat, the Baghdad thief, the Red Indian, the doctor's wife and more than likely others too, are individual spirits from the one soul. The soul has no solid form; it is outside the human body but can draw close and influence the spirit that is currently incarnated. Possibly this could explain how the experiences of other spirits within the soul have an effect upon the present spirit's incarnation. The spirit experiencing the current incarnation, on request, can contact the soul and therefore any spirit within it. In other words, if one would like to contact one's soul, techniques have been developed to assist in the process, should it not occur spontaneously. Since I was fourteen, the spirits who formed my soul were communicating with me, trying to help me to understand HIS soul and the incarnations that each spirit had experienced.

It is difficult to comprehend the concept that one is merely an aspect of the soul, and can be better explained by using the analogy that was used by St. Paul in the New Testament: –

'Would the hand say, because I am a hand, am I not of the body? Would the eye say; because I am an eye am I not of the body?'

It is understood that for the body to be whole it must contain many different parts, each having its own role to play. Likewise, for the soul to be whole it must contain many different spirits, each having had its own experiences and their own role to play.

My new understanding of the soul assisted me in understanding how the memories of Hassat and all the other incarnations I had experienced, during my journey, had been accessed and why they had been so important. The negative energy remaining from what is referred to as the karma of each lifetime was linked by my soul. The negative energy moved within my soul disrupting my present lifetime, making it impossible for me to achieve peace of mind.

I likened the soul to an orange with many segments - each segment representing a different incarnation – an individual spirit. One segment is not the orange, just as one spirit is not the soul. Every segment contained within a protective skin is the orange. Every spirit contained within an energy that is the soul.

In my attempt to forgive HIM over the years, I had studied the topics of Guilt, Fear, Forgiveness and Judgement. These topics had offered me an understanding and had assisted me in taking steps nearer to freeing myself of the past, but it did not go deep enough. It did not touch my soul. Forgiveness is, I had understood from childhood, being able to kiss and make up, being able to shake hands and put the past behind oneself. Often people continue to look upon forgiveness in the simple way of a young child, just as I had. When the child falls out with his/her friends an adult usually says something along the lines of: -

"Now shake hands and make friends!"

That is many peoples' earliest understanding of forgiveness. Someone we like and trust wrongs us, we argue and, agree to cease being friends and trusting that person. An adult arrives and insists that we must forgive each other, shake hands and like each other again. Adults often demand that this occurs instantly – or some form of privilege will be withheld until forgiveness occurs. This does not give the child time to evaluate their emotions and we therefore comply to 'keep someone else happy!'

After studying, I came to the conclusion that forgiveness is complete when one stops feeling angry and resentful towards another person who has wronged you: nothing more and nothing less. Forgiveness within the adult world does not mean that one has to come into physical contact with the person, who has hurt you, or to verbalize with them - and certainly not to become friends with them. However, these should remain as options.

'The Journey' had allowed me to forgive HIM for the wrongs he had committed and for what he did to me; it enabled me to stop feeling angry and resentful towards HIM. Nothing more and nothing less. But the forgiveness I had awarded HIM had freed me, had finally removed the black cloud that had hung above me since that fateful day. No matter what happened now, no matter if I was ill or well in the future, that heavy negative feeling could never ever return; I had been freed.

'The heaviest burdens that we carry are those that we cannot see – these we try to carry with dignity and yet they weigh us down and eat away at us from the inside out.'

The proof of the pudding was in the eating, Annie had said to the healer - and the proof of my pudding was that not only was I feeling more relaxed; I was happier and *definitely* free. Although I had been diagnosed with a progressive disease that had not been changed by the journey, no one could ever put back the black cloud that had previously hung heavily above me, blighting my life. I had been freed of the heavy, back cloud of negativity that had haunted me and, as a result, I knew that even with my health deteriorating, I would cope. I would live with it and through it, seeing it as one of life's challenges; embracing it, as opposed to retreating further into the darkness. The change in my attitude was in itself proof of the pudding.

Chapter Nine

A Wake-Up Call

9

Five long years prior to my trip to France, I had received a wake-up call. One that I had ignored or rather *acknowledged* and then ran away from, hidden from...

My mother-in-law had been searching for some time for a suitable house to move to and I had accompanied her on numerous occasions to view properties. One property was perfect. It had everything she needed, including a small, neat garden and my mother-in-law immediately put in an offer, which was accepted. The house purchase was proceeding quickly without a hitch until one morning I received a call from my mother-in-law, who was in tears. The gentleman who was selling the property had had a change of heart and had suddenly and unexpectedly, decided not to move after all. The only words of comfort I could offer to my mother-in-law were that when the same thing had happened to my husband and I, a much better house was waiting for us just around the corner.

I continued to help my mother-in-law to view properties, however nothing was suitable. Then early one Sunday morning, I received a phone call from my mother-in-law, who was obviously very excited. She informed me that she had found a perfect house at a perfect price. It was at the other end of town - a small mid-terrace house with two bedrooms and a compact garden to the rear. There was only a small chain and so the process of purchasing the property sailed through this time without a hitch.

Within weeks the day came for the move to take place. I, my husband Ian and two of his aunts and two uncles gathered in the road outside the new house. The group waited and waited; the removal van arrived and waited with us. A message then arrived from my mother-in-law to say that there had been a slight hitch, one that had to be sorted prior to the exchange taking place and the keys being handed over. The process would take about an hour!

While awaiting the keys the removal men sat back in their van, Ian's relations sat on a low wall and chatted while Ian and I sat in our car. The mood was one of frustration because evening was fast approaching and everyone was keen to unload the van and unpack the boxes before nightfall. Time ticked by and one hour was quickly turning into two hours and still there was no sign of the elusive keys!

Suddenly, I heard a voice that made every hair stand on end; a voice that made my world stand still; a voice that catapulted me back to my childhood. The voice belonged to a man who was talking to Ian's relations, kindly asking if they would like a cup of tea! The man introduced himself as the new next-door-neighbour of my mother-in-law! The man was HIM. A few years older, a few hairs greyer, a few pounds heavier but there was no mistaking the same voice; it was the same man...

I froze, with my senses buzzing with alertness preparing me for flight, allowing me to run away and to escape and yet at the same time I felt as though every muscle of my body had been paralysed by fear, shock, horror and disbelief.

The town in which we lived consisted of about twenty-thousand houses and I could not believe that against all the odds, HE lived in the house next door to my mother-in-law! I had not set eyes upon him more than twice since the case had finished at Crown Court and wasn't even aware that he still lived in the town. I tried to rationalize, how could this possibly have happened, how he could live next door? As my mind tried to evaluate what to do next, panic rose in my throat and tears pricked in my eyes. I just stared blankly out of the car window trying to take stock of the situation.

Also recognising HIM, Ian turned to me and compassionately asked,

"What do you want to do now?" He gently broke into my thoughts.

"Take me to see my mum!" I said, suddenly having the need to be held by Annie's supportive arms.

Ian drove my across town without speaking a word as silent tears cascaded down my cheeks. When we arrived at the centre where my mother was that afternoon, I composed myself before entering. Ian sat down on the chair next to me and held my hand tightly while we waited for Annie to finish talking to the people she was conversing with. We sat in silence, for Ian was at a loss as to what he could say. He too could not believe what had just occurred. Annie looked up and saw us sitting silently at the back of the room. Perplexed as to why we were there instead of unpacking boxes, Annie approached us.

"Is everything alright?" she enquired, puzzled.

At that moment my resolve to be composed disintegrated and loud uncontrollable sobs began to escape. Annie ushered me into a small-unoccupied room, as the sobs grew louder and louder seeming to be coming from the core of my being. Knowing by Ian's expressions that whatever troubled her daughter was a personal issue and not one directly concerning them both, Annie hugged me and waited for the sobs to subside.

Finally, after some considerable time I was able to speak. However, to actually verbalize what I had realized that afternoon, made me feel physically sick. My stomach turned at the obscenity of the situation and I retched. Eventually I managed to force out the words,

"He...He...HE lives next door!" I finally shouted.

Ian silently mouthed HIS name to Annie and then looked back down at his feet.

"Oh my God, NO!" was all that Annie could say in response.

After spending some time with my mother and drinking a calming cup of tea, I gathered strength and became defiant. As Annie and Ian sat one each side of me wondering what to do next, I, having gained strength from being away from the situation and along with their support, announced that it was time to return to my mother-in-law and help unpack the boxes!

When we returned to the house, my mother-in-law had just arrived with the keys, the removal van doors were being unlocked and Ian's relatives were all eagerly gathered around the front door awaiting entry. There was no time for anyone to question our whereabouts, as Ian quickly chaperoned me into the house. Ian had instructed me to stay inside the house and as he went outside to assist the others carrying boxes from the removal van, I settled myself in the kitchen unpacking crockery.

With so much to get on with before dark, I almost forgot about the man who was lurking a few inches away, the other side of the wall. I remained working alone in the kitchen whilst hearing the others going in and out of the house and up and down the stairs. I heard the front door close and suddenly it went quiet as it seemed everyone had gone upstairs. Bending down to put the last of the plates in the base unit, I heard the doorbell ring. Someone answered it and then I heard HIS voice,

"Shall I put the tray down in the kitchen then?" HE asked, "I have put sugar on the tray too as I didn't know if you would have found yours yet!" he continued, HIS voice getting nearer.

I felt my cheeks flush as once again panic took me over. Frantically my eyes darted around the tiny kitchen, there was no more than four feet by three feet of standing room and HE was fast approaching the door. Quickly I threw myself against the door holding the handle as rigid as I could. HE had been too strong for me once and I was not going to let that happen again! I held the door handle tightly, as if my life depended upon it. Time stood still as a thousand scenarios played out in my head. At last the moment arrived and I felt him pushing the handle down...once...twice...three times and then,

"The handle seems a bit stiff and I can't do much about it with this tray balanced in the other hand, so I will just leave it here!" He said releasing the door handle.

I breathed a sigh of relief - I was safe again! Then I heard HIS voice once more,

"Have I made enough drinks?" he asked.

"Actually," My mother-in-law replied, mentally counting her helpers and the cups. "We could do with another one - Oh and don't put any milk in it because Wendy takes her tea black."

Repulsed at the thought of drinking anything that had been prepared by those menacing, probing, despicable hands I shouted rudely, through the tightly shut kitchen door,

"I DON'T WANT A DRINK!"

I remained in the kitchen, my body wedged against the door, locking me into my protective cell, while the other helpers selected their drinks and chatted freely with HIM. I knew that Ian would be guarding the other side of the door and yet as I stood there in the tiny room I felt desperately alone and vulnerable again. I slid down the door to the floor and as I sat with my back firmly against it and my knees bent, I held my head in my hands. I felt as vulnerable as I had felt that fateful day in my childhood. As vulnerable as I had felt standing alone in the witness box in that stark courtroom. Tears began to flow down my cheeks. As the tears flowed, I thought to myself

'I am an adult with a home and family of my own so why have I allowed what has happened this afternoon to have transported me back in time and why do I once again feel so alone, vulnerable and scared.'

Try as I might, I did not have the strength to fight the emotions that had once been buried but were now surfacing. As I sat motionless on the floor of the tiny kitchen, I permitted the silent tears to cascade onto my clothes. At last I heard him leave, taking the tray of empty cups with him. For some time I remained in my safe haven, desiring to remain alone.

'This is how it is going to be!' I thought glumly, 'He is going to keep popping in and out of this house, playing the good neighbour role...I won't ever be safe here... He is going to haunt me again. Is he going to ruin the lovely relationship that I have with my mother-in-law?'

Finally, the day was drawing to an end and in an attempt to explain my strange behaviour, Ian told his uncle about the man next door. The uncle was weary after an exhausting day and after making appropriately compassionate remarks asked Ian not to tell his mother until the next day. However, there was one person who I knew I must tell immediately – my sister-in-law, the mother of two children, the youngest of whom was an eight year old, very trusting, pretty little girl. After informing her, I knew that she thought I was over reacting, possibly even being silly. My sister-in-law didn't seem to understand that this MAN who had abused me was still the same person. I felt exposed as she hung up the phone. I related the feelings that I was experiencing, once again to the court case, and of having to explain to strangers what he had done to me. Again tears came, I knew I had done the right thing in alerting my sister-in-law and I knew it was important to protect my niece so why, I wondered, did I feel so wretched?

The mood was sombre; when Ian and I returned home that evening both of us were mentally and physically exhausted. As expected, a restless night followed. Vivid dreams pushed their way into my sleep and in the morning I decided it was time to sit my son down and reveal my past to him. I, and in fact, no one else, could be sure that HE had not sexually abused boys as well as the eight other girls that were listed as victims in the court case.

Sitting myself on the sofa next to my young son, I slowly turned to look at him, "Mummy needs to talk to you about something very important," I began, "And I need you to pay attention...when I was a teenager," I continued, "A nasty man hurt mummy! The man, who hurt mummy, lives next door to Grandma now."

As I paused, my son looked at me wide-eyed. I knew exactly what he was thinking and so explained further,

"You don't need to worry about Grandma because he is really, really nice to grown-ups but nasty to children, so…" I continued seriously, "You have to promise mummy and daddy that even if he is nice to you, you must NEVER talk to him or go into his house."

My son sat for some time, motionless - just staring at me. It was obviously difficult for him, as it would be for any child to imagine anyone hurting their mummy. He was upset for both his mother and his grandmother,

"What did he do to you mummy?" he finally asked tearfully.

"That doesn't matter now. I am fine but what matters is that he doesn't hurt you my darling!" I finished feeling that there was no need to take the conversation further.

Mother and son had a long, silent hug and I thought to myself how wrong it was to have to tell my young child such an awful thing. The ordeal was not yet over. I knew that I had to inform my mother-in-law next, for it would be up to her to ensure all of the children's safety when they visited and were in her care. It was a conversation that I dreaded, especially as my mother-in-law had had a very bad year and was overjoyed at having found the perfect home at last and with, in her opinion, friendly, helpful neighbours.

After leaving our son with my parents, Ian and I made our way down to my mother-in-law's new house. On the way we discussed exactly how best to break the awful news. On arrival, I felt my heart begin to beat faster and harder in my chest; my palms became clammy as I wrung my hands together. I stared at the closed door next to my mother-in-law's, expecting it to burst open any second.

"Come on," Ian coaxed gently, "Mum will understand!"

He walked around the car and opened the door for me and then holding out his hand in encouragement, he smiled reassuringly. I grabbed his hand and held it as if it were my lifeline from a sinking ship. Quickly, silently, we walked down the path and were greeted by my mother-in-law, smiling broadly.

"Come in, come in!" she welcomed, turning to enter the house, "Tea?" she asked, glancing over her shoulder.

I looked around the room, each box had been unpacked and each item found a home. It would have appeared to those that didn't already know that mother-in-law had lived there for years. It was a perfect house, already a home. The new house was the perfect size for her and her little Yorkshire Terrier, Harry. Mother-in-law re-entered the room and set the tea tray on the coffee table, beaming as she surveyed all that was hers.

Once tea and pleasantries were over, I knew that it was time - time to shatter my mother-in-law's new-found happiness. I felt like a master about to order an unsuspecting trusted pet to be put down.

"Mum!" I started, glancing at the door, half expecting HIM to burst through it at any moment bearing gifts.

"Mum, I have something that I have to tell you!" I began reluctantly. I was glad that I had shared with her what had happened to me many years before, as it spared me the ordeal of having to go through it all now.

"You know that I told you that I was sexually abused when I was younger, and that it went to court and everything?" I began, pausing to look at my mother-in-law's perplexed expression.

"Well," I continued, "The man who did it, he, he, lives next door to you!" I blurted out.

I looked to Ian for support and then back to my mother-in-law praying for understanding. The three of us sat in the lovely, new house in silence for some considerable time. Neither one of us knew what to say, each grappling to find words to suit the occasion. Just when it seemed that we would be stuck in our silent world forever, the loud shrill of the telephone broke into our thoughts and snapped us back to the moment. Mother-in-law walked solemnly into the hallway and picked up the receiver.

"Oh, hello!" I heard her say.

I turned to my husband and in a hushed voice asked,

"Do you think that I have done the right thing in telling her?"

"Yes, you had to - you had no choice!" he replied firmly.

Finally, mother-in-law returned and informed us that the call had been from her sister. She then went on to explain that she had shared the information I had just revealed to her, with her sibling. I sat quietly, waiting for her to continue, expecting her to have offered words of compassion, words of understanding perhaps. Wanting, needing to be understood; to be reassured; to be... important!

"What did she say?" I asked when it seemed obvious that the response was not forthcoming.

"She said," commenced mother-in-law, "That I am the one who lives here and not you. I can't move again!" She finished looking pitifully at me.

I felt as though a missile had just careered into my abdomen. I had already realized that unfortunate as it may be, it was out of the question for my mother-in-law to move again, but had never-the-less expected support, compassion, even love from my family-in-law.

"I never expected you to move!" was all that I could say in response.

Ian went and collected our son, returned with fish and chips, to find that the last box that had been hiding upstairs had finally been unpacked and finally every item now had a home. We ate the meal and bravely I joined in as we toasted the new house together. Finally, my little family left to return to the safety of our own home once more.

That night the nightmare came again. The same one that had haunted me periodically throughout my life…the nightmare that I referred to as the 'What if' Nightmare! What would have happened if HIS dog had not barked on that fateful day, allowing me to finally escape?! In the nightmare, the dog doesn't bark. In the silence of the early hours of the morning, immersed in darkness, I wrestled with the demons of my mind, tortured by the thoughts flowing through my head. I was alone and fully awakened by the nightmare again!

Surprisingly, life went on and the normality of routine took over again. The nightmares subsided and I managed to block out recent events, choosing to speak to my mother-in-law over the phone rather than to visit. A few weeks later I received a call from mother-in-law inviting us to join her for Sunday lunch. Without thinking the invitation through, I graciously accepted. Then throwing myself into everyday life soon forgot about the commitment I had made. The week rushed past and the week end once again was upon us. In the supermarket it suddenly dawned on me that there was no need to shop for Sunday's food as we were expected at my mother-in-laws.

Having remembered the invitation, I began to think about physically going to the house, about how I would have to sit on the sofa, knowing that he was sitting on his sofa a mere few inches behind me, on the other side of the wall. As night fell, the thoughts were once again racing through my head and I could feel myself becoming more and more short-tempered. I heard myself snapping at my husband and being impatient with my son. I felt myself retreating into my protective shell. The night was plagued with nightmares and visions, probabilities, possibilities and assumptions once again.

When morning finally arrived, I was exhausted and even more fraught with fear. I went through the motions of getting my son ready to visit his grandmother, until I found myself sitting next to my husband in the front seat of the car travelling towards my mother-in-law's house. As the roads led me nearer, I felt bile rise to my throat. I heard my heart pounding ferociously against my chest wall and my breath entering and exiting my nose at a quicker pace as my fate awaited me.

No sightings occurred and the meal went without a hitch. It would have seemed, to anyone looking in, just like any other Sunday family mealtime and yet the tension hung in the air like smog above the streets of London on an autumn evening. The sound of the unspoken words became unbearably prominent, until finally it was time for us to return home.

Again, life quickly returned to normal, until the next time that we had to visit that fateful house. Then the nightmares would commence, the short-temperedness would take over and the tension would rise. After several such visits I broke down, "I can't do it; I just can't do it anymore. I have tried, and God knows I have tried but I just can't do it. I cannot go to that house again. I can't keep putting myself through this ordeal time and time again!" I finished, relieved to have finally verbalized what was in my heart.

"It is OK. You don't have to go anymore!" Ian comforted me.

We both knew that mother-in-law would be upset, and that there was a chance she would not understand. We knew that the rest of the family would probably talk about how silly I was being, but I didn't care. I felt only total relief. It was, after all, my life and I had to ultimately do what was best for me and my own little family.

I avoided going to the house and mother-in-law stopped inviting us all. Guilt often crept in, but I had decided that it was better to experience occasional guilt than frequently experience the avalanche of other emotions that had been bombarding me. I was, after all, conversing on the phone with mother-in-law on an almost daily basis and she often visited me at my own home. Life would have been perfect once more if only mother-in-law did not insist upon mentioning HIM every day.

"HE is so helpful, do you know what he did for me today?" she quizzed one day, "HE offered to trim all my climbing roses back for winter. He knows I could never manage to do it on my own!" she answered.

Then, on another occasion, "HE is so good to me. He knocked on the door this morning to see if I was alright because I was late opening the curtains!" She twittered, "It is such a comfort knowing I have good neighbours!"

I felt as though I had been betrayed and despised the thought that my mother-in-law, whom I believed, should have been standing alongside me in the battle against this evil man had chosen, actually chosen, to befriend him. To befriend him even after I had poured out my heart, told mother-in-law how he had once hurt me so badly, was almost too big an insult to bare. I kept my thoughts to myself as I listened to mother-in-law relay the stories of this 'knight in shining armour.' One day mother-in-law stopped talking and looked at my face, the expression upon it must have portrayed my feelings.

"Look," mother-in-law began, "I know you don't like HIM, but I can only speak as I find, and HE has always been very good to me!" she finished.

"I know you don't like him!" I wanted to scream back at her, "I know you don't like HIM, of course I don't like HIM! After what he did to me how could I possibly like HIM? After what I have told you, how could you possibly like HIM?" I wanted to rage back at her.

But from her point of view, she spoke the truth, I thought. HE had always been extremely good to her. But the words mother-in-law spoke that day cut me to the core. Was she saying that in the light of how well HE had treated her, she didn't believe me or was she saying that she did believe me but that it didn't matter, I mused? From that moment on, mother-in-law still spoke of HIM but ceased using HIS name, replacing it with – 'my next-door-neighbour' - as if, somehow, that took the pain away...

This was the wake-up call that I had needed to face my past and the demons that lurked there. For some obscure reason the universe had offered me the opportunity to deal with the emotions and the debilitating hurt that had found residence deep within my soul. Instead of accepting this gift from the universe, I had sought to bury the past even deeper; deeper into the core of my being.

Instead of viewing the circumstances as an opportunity to move towards freedom, I saw it as being part of a personal vendetta; I saw it as the whole universe being against me. I saw it as a series of events that gave rise to stronger feelings of hatred, of fear and of vulnerability within me than the feelings that I had previously harboured. I saw it as a series of events that wrenched me from the bosom of my husband's family and created a barrier between us. This was a series of events that made me feel betrayed by my beloved mother-in-law. A series of unfair, cruel, vindictive events set to torture me more. And I failed to acknowledge the wake-up call - I chose to ignore it and I ran; I hid...

Chapter Ten

The Ending Came

A month after returning from France, Lindsay had given me a copy of Brandon Bay's book, in which Brandon told how she discovered the Journey Therapy and how it had helped many people, including herself, by releasing past traumas. She explained how by removing the negative memory that is held within a cell, physical health problems could be eradicated, and how changes could occur deep inside the person just as they had with me, offering freedom from the darkness that had hung over them. I settled myself in bed to read the book, smiling to myself. It was probably the case that people usually read the book and then sought out a therapist, I thought, eager to compare the experience of the author with that of my own. As I read through the first few chapters, I found it compelling reading and was glad that my own journeywork was complete. I usually avoided reading but found that I wanted to peruse this book all night. At half past midnight I finally switched off the bedside lamp, giving in to the sleepiness that was beginning to blur my vision.

The night passed quickly and the alarm for my husband to get up for work broke into my deep slumber. I yawned and stretched, my throat was dry and I made my way out of bed and down stairs to the kitchen to make some tea. The sun was already high in the sky and bringing its warmth to the thick curtains that were attempting to shut it out. I parted them and then thrust open the window. I took a gulp of the fresh morning air before settling myself back in bed with my tea and picking up the book. I glanced at the radio alarm clock – 5.50am it glowed. I had two hours before it was time to get up. Two hours of reading I smiled, snuggling down into the duvet. Never before had I had this luxury, never before had I been so wide-awake at this hour of the morning.

I quickly read on to the part where Brandon shut herself away in silent retreat, for five days in order to experience the emotions that were still held within her cells and stopping her tumour from healing completely. She gave details of how she sat in her armchair and allowed her suppressed emotions and memories to surface. She explained how she fell through the layers of emotions until she felt the utter despair that was in the centre. Brandon then explained how she stayed with the feeling and allowed herself to fall into the pit of despair, deeper and deeper and how finally deep within the pit she discovered bliss. Her own bliss!

As I read the chapter, emotions began to surface within me and I allowed myself to feel them. Realizing that my soul was responding to something outside my conscious understanding, I put the book down. Tears began forming behind my eyes as I lay down in bed again and closed my eyes. I focused upon the feeling that I was experiencing and realized that it was the feeling of guilt and with it came images from the past. I was instantly transported back to when I was fourteen years old. I was a shy schoolgirl, living a sheltered life within an idyllic family, in a relatively small seaside town on the southeast coast.

I had just told my parents that my friend's step dad had touched me inappropriately and they had been angry. I hadn't wanted them to make any kind of fuss and my parents had agreed as long as I promised never to go to my friend's house again, that they would not involve the police. It was a hard promise to make, because I had been very close to my friend for as long as I could remember but on the other hand, I never wanted to set eyes on HIM again. I already knew that he had a violent temper; I remembered that he beat my friend's mum breaking her ribs and then had used a spade to smash up the house. I remembered how HE had done all that just because his dinner wasn't cooked to his satisfaction. I knew that he had hit my friend's brother with a belt often and I inwardly had always been scared of him. Now I just wanted to forget the whole business and never come into contact with him again!

Suddenly, without warning, I found I had been propelled forwards a few months in time and was now riding my bike. It would have seemed to onlookers that I was a normal school girl riding my bicycle on a sunny Saturday afternoon, on my way to my friend's house. This was to be no normal afternoon. I had not told my parents where I was going, of course, and I did feel guilty. As a shy teenager, I never went against my parent's wishes; I was a good daughter and certainly never kept secrets of this magnitude from them. I glanced over my shoulder as if my guilt was drawing attention to myself. No one knew where I was going, except me and my friend.

The fact of the matter was, that I was missing my friend and had made so many excuses that I now felt that the only choice I had was to either lose our special friendship forever or go to my friend's house. Telling my friend the truth was out of the question.

As far as I was aware, my friend loved her stepfather and it would hurt her too much to know the truth about him. She may not believe me and think I was making it up as part of some childish agenda. I chose to keep my secret and therefore 'protect' my friend and preserve our friendship. When we had made the arrangement to meet that Saturday afternoon, my friend had said that she and her brother would be there with their mother but that HE would be at work.

I felt uneasy as I dismounted and parked my bike at the side of the house. My heart was pounding guiltily in my chest as I gingerly knocked on the door. My friend's brother opened the door and greeted me warmly. As I stepped into the hall I was convinced that he could see my chest pounding madly. I bent down to remove my shoes and picking them up, followed him through the kitchen and into the dining room, where I expected to see my friend.

"Where is your sister?" I asked, surprised not to have seen her by now.

"Oh, she has gone to the shop to get a video" was the casual reply.

Apprehension turned to excitement; not many people had video players at the time and the novelty almost made the deceit worthwhile. I sat down in an armchair beside the coal fire in the dining room and chatted with my friend's brother. Quickly I learned that their mother had been called into work and wouldn't be home till the evening.

I looked at my watch it was two-thirty.

"Hello, nice to see you again!" a voice smugly cut into our conversation.

I froze, my heart rate increased, my mouth felt dry, my face flushed and I began to tremble. I opened my mouth but no words would come out. We stared at each other in silence, silence that allowed a million unspoken words to pass between us, and then in order to break away from his stare I commenced a conversation with my friend's brother, while silently praying for my friend to return. HE watched the two of us conversing for a while, maybe revelling at the ingeniousness of his plan and then exuding his power over the boy calmly looked at him and said,

"You had better go now!" Then continued,

"Your Nan is expecting you and you are late!"

My friend's brother jumped up in response and quickly obeyed, obviously perplexed by the order but not in the habit of arguing with HIM.

"I'd better go now too!" I exclaimed panicking and bending forward to retrieve my shoes.

"No! Your friend will be here in a minute. You wait!" He said firmly.

I wanted to go, I wanted to escape, but I couldn't risk him getting angry or losing his temper. There was no one there to protect me. My friend's brother was not strong enough physically or mentally to fight HIM. I quickly assessed the situation and realized that my plan that afternoon had been for no-one to know where I was, which meant no-one would look for me here and I had no idea how long my friend would be or if by chance her mother would return from work early - although HE obviously did!

I sat in the chair motionless, thoughts rushing through my head. I knew that I was now in a very bad situation. I was a sensible young girl and I knew that I was very vulnerable but also that I must not do anything to antagonize him. The young boy packed up his things, put on his coat and shoes and said good-bye to me and left.

I was now alone with HIM. My friend was obviously going to be some time as I had discovered from the conversation I had had with my friends' brother that HE had given her a list of other items to also get from the shop - items I knew that would not be easy to find! My eyes darted around the room, if one ever wanted to know what terror was like, I thought – this was it! At that moment I felt fear alerting every cell of my body. Thoughts raced through my mind as I tried out a variety of excuses and escape routes. Finally realizing that there was no escape from the situation that I found myself in, the situation that I had put myself in, the situation that my deceit had placed me in, I resigned myself to my fate. Fear gave me the illusion that time had stood still and then, as I sat paralysed by the fear I was experiencing, he slowly walked over and sat on the dining chair that was positioned next to my armchair.

"This is it!" I thought as my young frame tensed.

Now HE moved quickly and even though I knew what to expect, it had come as a shock. HE leant over me, forcefully pushing me backwards, trapping me in the high-backed armchair – our eyes met and I held his gaze. I desperately transmitted a silent, pleading message as we stared into each other's eyes for what seemed like an eternity. HE received my plea, understood the fear I was feeling and revelled in the power HE exuded over his victim. HIS eyes remained fixed on mine as HIS hands expertly manoeuvred across my young body.

I dug my sharp nails, as hard as I could, into the back of one of his rugged hands and tugged frantically at it. HE was a grown man, HE was strong and I, a young slender teenager, did not have the strength to remove them. I tried desperately again, this time pulling one finger at a time, bending it backwards, hoping the pain it caused would stop him from causing me anymore pain but to no avail. HIS hands groping and exploring my body were too strong, too solid and too determined for a fourteen-year-old girl. In that moment I knew that I had a choice. I could either let him do whatever HE wanted to do without challenging him and risking making him angry or I could try to fight harder and risk him losing his temper as I had seen him do on a number of occasions before.

If he didn't get his own way, I thought he may even kill me. A picture of my loving family flashed through my mind and as John Lennon's 'Woman' played on the radio I waited, eyes fixed on his, I prayed he would stop. A satisfied smirk spread across his face as I gave in to his strength, resigning myself to my fate. At that moment HE knew the battle was over and HE had won.

Finally HIS dog barked, and thinking that someone was coming to the door, HE stood up and then calmly walked upstairs. HE had changed me forever and then just calmly walked away! Seizing the opportunity, not even stopping to straighten my clothes I grabbed my shoes and ran out of the back door. I leapt onto my bike and pedalled barefoot as fast as I could. My parents, I knew, were out and so I rode as fast as I could to the nearest safe place. As my grandmother opened the front door in response to my frantic knocking and repeated ringing of the bell, I rushed inside bringing with me my bike, a necessary precaution, I felt, in case he was out looking for me and saw it parked outside.

Safe, at my grandmother's house, I fell into the comfort of her outstretched arms unable to speak. I shook with fear and rage and disbelief. How could a grown-up do this to a child, it was beyond my comprehension. My grandmother saw the tears running down my cheeks as at last I managed to sob out the gist of what had happened to me. Sense prevailed and my grandmother, knowing where my parents would be, phoned them asking them to come immediately. I was horrified as I now realized that I had to tell my parents! I realized, they would be angry, because they had made me promise never to go there again and I had given them my word. Now I had paid the ultimate price for my disobedience. I had no-one to blame but myself. I realized that the wretchedness that I was experiencing now was all of my own making and, I concluded, I was entitled to no sympathy and deserved the anger of my parents that was soon to come.

Of course my parents had not been angry with me. They had comforted, nurtured me and loved me. The police were fantastic as well; bizarrely to me, no one seemed to blame me except myself! With the support of my family and the police officers, slowly I began to heal.

It was a completely different story, when I arrived at court. It was then that the blame came. His lawyers blamed me. Across the open courtroom, in front of strangers – both men and women - they had blamed me, implied that at the time of 'the incident' I was not merely an innocent child. Instead they had tried to paint a picture to those in the courtroom of me as a 'girl about town' as if, *had that been true*, it would have made his behaviour acceptable!

While the lawyers humiliated me, asking questions and demanding graphic answers, HE sat there smirking at me, silently laughing at my attempts to control the tears that the questions and subsequent memories provoked. HIS eyes entered into a tormenting dialogue with me across the courtroom as the avalanche of questions from condescending lawyers continued. The pain, the humiliation, the embarrassment at having to tell a room full of strangers what had happened to me, was all my own fault I knew!

My father sat in the courtroom listening to everything. My mother, too ill, following recent surgery to be there, waited at home silently suffering. All of this was my own fault I knew. The shame, the embarrassment, the suffering - I was guilty, I deserved it! I broke his stare and my eyes skipped from one face to another across the courtroom and vivid flashes of memories of that fateful day strobed across my mind. The same vivid memories that haunted my dreams and would continue to haunt my dreams for a quarter of a century to come.

As I lay on my bed, tears flowing, I felt the despair and the pain yet again. I wanted it to stop; I didn't want to remember anything about it. The events of that fateful day played out in my mind now, slowly, not sparing a single detail. For a moment I felt angry, I thought that Faye had 'cured' me of this pain and yet here it was more powerful than ever. Never before had I allowed myself to remember in such detail, to transport myself back to that fateful Saturday afternoon when my idyllic childhood had ended. As the familiar, heavy, crushing feelings consumed my body, somewhere from my subconscious I recalled Brandon's words: -

'You must let yourself fall into the pit of despair'.

I was scared, I knew the pain that was lurking deep within that pit and yet I knew that I had to trust my soul. It was, after all, my soul that had brought me to this point and I couldn't let it down now. Taking a deep breath and sniffing as I stifled a sob I submitted to the feelings and entered into the pit, my own sea of emotional despair.

It was not how I had expected it to be. I had been prepared for a quick drop, to feel as though I was falling from a great height into a pit of negativity but instead found myself gently floating through the blackness. I could hear voices as I drifted down. They were all my own I registered, my own desperate cries for help.

"Help me... please help me... pleeeeaze... pleeeeaze!" the pitiful voices cried out of the blackness.

I felt afraid, my heart rate increased, my breathing became rapid and my body clammy.

"Help me... help me...!" The voices continued.

Suddenly seeing the blackness and recognising the voices for what they were, I heard myself respond, "I don't need help!" I whispered, then gaining strength, "I don't need help," I shouted to myself, "I am doing this on my own!"

I was still afraid, but as time went on and I continued to float deeper and deeper into the pit, a new feeling began to emerge from deep within my core. It was trust. I was beginning to trust myself. I had let myself down once very badly, gone against my instincts, against my parents and had therefore sub-consciously vowed never to trust myself again as a result and yet, bizarrely, here in this pit of despair, drifting through my own hell I found I was able to trust myself again.

Then there it was! Instantly as if in response to my dawning trust, it appeared. It was not as I had imagined, a pinprick of light that would draw me closer and closer, but light that was brighter than the sun itself and a light that all at once filled every corner of my hell; an all-encompassing brightness that brought with it such calm, such joy, such peace; such peace. I had at last discovered that which my soul craved – I had found bliss and I had found it alone.

From Behind Bars The Sun Emerges

This, I realized, was what it had all been about - all the tireless searching. For years I had outwardly sought that which was all the time within myself. Years had been wasted waiting for someone to help save me and yet it had been there, hidden within me all the time. I began to laugh and cry at the same time, as I opened my eyes. I had completely forgotten that I was still lying on my bed and that it would soon be time to get up. Time had stood still but this time it had offered me the space to heal myself and I had taken it!

For a few minutes I lay motionless, allowing the tears to fall and yet still smiling and laughing at the same time. Just as the moment passed and I finished dabbing my tears, Alex entered the room;

"Are you getting up mum?" he questioned.
"Yes, I'm just coming" I replied.

Chapter Eleven

Pause for Thought

Later that day, alone in my room, I took out my journal and wrote: -

'I have been into the depths of hell. I have seen the dark demons that lurk there. Once the demons catch sight of you, they cling to you - grab at you. Dragging you down and down, again and again, back into the bowels of hell each time you try to escape. Who are these demons and where is hell? Demons are the outward manifestation of negative thoughts and feelings. Hell exists, not in the fiery core at the centre of the earth, but within each of us, occupying the same space as heaven.

'Heaven and hell are nothing but states of mind. If one focuses on negative thoughts, feelings and experiences – a state of hell is created. Likewise, if one focuses upon positive thoughts, feelings and experiences, a state of heaven is created. Both heaven and hell are either conscious or subconscious choices, made by an individual to surrender and put their trust in that which they feel. We allow ourselves to be immersed by our emotional focus, be it good or bad. Both heaven and hell are addictive.

'With help, one can claw out of the depths of hell; but until one allows oneself to reach the gates of heaven and decides to walk through, it lurks like a rain cloud waiting to shower down upon one; dampening the progress that has been made.

'Having experienced both hell and heaven I have now made a choice to reside in a state of heaven! All that I needed was to release my manifested demons, to shake off the dark cloud that hung heavily above me, enabling me to discover the key to heaven lying exposed within my heart.

'As I grasped that key, I made the conscious decision to unlock heaven. As I did so, heaven opened its gates and laid its riches in front of me. My being had at that moment, become immersed in bliss, as heaven embraced me. My focus changed. From within the centre of each cell, I began to release the power that the memory of negative experiences had had over my mind. I let go of the negative thoughts, feelings and emotions that had manifested and, as this occurred at cellular level, the demons that had silently clung to me, hidden within my soul, lost their grip, their power, their claim and they fell away - freeing me.

'As I continued journeying deep within my soul, there at the centre, I found glowing, the Essence of The Divine. As the demons fell away and my spirit was cleansed, the glow of my own Divine Spark re-ignited and instantly illuminated every corner of my body, mind, spirit and soul. As heaven opened its gates to me, I walked through with my head held high; proud and strong. I felt clean and worthy of the honour that I had bestowed upon myself. Joy, calm and bliss are mine to experience as long as I choose to. Yes, BLISS is finally mine!

'My health may not be perfect, I may still suffer the associated symptoms of the diseases I suffer from; but the dark cloud of negativity that once rested above my head is gone forever! No longer do I feel its oppression, its restriction, its evil grip! I am finally free!!!

'Yes Bliss is finally mine!'

Chapter Twelve

Another Twist in the Tale!

Several mediums over many years had told me that in a previous incarnation, I had turned to the dark side; had used magic – black magic. Deep down, somehow, I had always been aware of that. I wasn't ashamed, or fearful of it, I just accepted it as something that had once been. Some mediums even went as far as to describe others from that lifetime that had joined forces with me and had worked together, perfecting the magic. Over time I had been made aware that all but one of the evil group had incarnated in this lifetime together in order to reverse the negative energies that we had summoned eons ago. One had remained in the spirit realm to guide us, to find each other and to assist us in making amends.

Over time it had been revealed to me that in that lifetime I had worked alongside strong, powerful magicians, who were incarnated in this lifetime as my mother, Annie, the most inoffensive, giving person one could ever wish to meet. Sean, an ex-member of The Searchers Group, who was an empathic healer and a spiritual soul. He had first met Annie and I when he moved next door to my father's mother and had later chosen to work spiritually alongside us. Also there was Bob, a man who had worked with my father Alan, and had taken him under his wing when he started working in the laboratory. Bob had understood mediumship and energy and had enjoyed working within a development circle. He had been the person who introduced my mother and I to meditation practices. The final member of the powerful group was Brenda, one of Annie and my closest friends - a deeply spiritual friend with whom we had shared many profound experiences. We were introduced to each other again, *via* my father, as he had socialised with Brenda's late husband. I had spoken over the years, with each of them in turn and they each were able to identify with what I had been told. It seemed that Alan was instrumental at reuniting the ex-magicians!

My Dad

I have also glimpsed into that incarnation on a few occasions. I recall seeing myself as a strong, muscular, healthy man of about thirty, standing on what I can only describe as an altar at the front of a large temple-like structure. I am dressed in clean bright white cloth, which is swathed across my fit virile body. I have thick gold bangles on each wrist that serve to secure the cloth, giving the appearance of sleeves. A chunky, gold-barred necklace is draped around my neck and, thin, brown leather laces from my gladiator style sandals climb my bulging calves. My jet-black hair is cut into a square shoulder length bob and thick black makeup frames my eyes and extends outward towards my temples.

I know that I am powerful; that I am revered and, that I am feared! In the moment in which I find myself, I enjoy the emotions that I am experiencing and have the desire to experience more. To me, at the moment within that incarnation that I find myself, power is the most important thing. In fact, power appears to be all that is important. As I stand upon the altar, in front of a large audience, I lift both arms and stretch them upwards as if motioning to the assembled crowd to be silent. The chattering that had been present ceases and, hardly a breath can be heard.

I turn to face a large font just in front and, to the right of me. I click my fingers loudly, whilst abruptly pointing towards it: as I do so, I release a small amount of grey powder with coarse gritty bits mixed with it. As the powder meets the font, the liquid contained within it spontaneously ignites. A gasp is released from the crowd as they prostrate themselves onto the ground. I turn, as if to smugly gain approval of the five men standing against the wall a few feet behind me. They each step forward so that they are parallel to me, as if they too are claiming their place in the proceedings.

The group of six men (including me), I knew, held the most important position in the community and in all the communities in the area. The people were afraid to do anything without the approval of these powerful magicians, whom they believed to be vessels of the 'gods'. It became clear to me that in that lifetime, I had the knowledge of how to manipulate energy. I realized that I had been responsible for teaching my co-workers to do the same. Once they had mastered the energy, I had taught them how to use that ability for their own gain.

As I now stood proudly on the altar with my colleagues, in front of the people, *my* people, I exuded dominance over them. I was making all of their lives as unpleasant as I was able. Many were hungry; many had no homes, many were afraid to even think for themselves. I was all powerful. I was who I wanted to be!

Whenever I returned from this vision, I felt uneasy. I hated the thought that I had used the power of the universe in such a negative way. That I had been responsible for the suffering of so many. (Maybe this accounts for the reason that I am so intent upon teaching others how to use positive energies, in my current lifetime.) I tried to push it to the back of my mind and focus upon harnessing the energy of the universe in a positive way, to help other people. In my workshops and classes, I had always ensured that as far as possible I explained the myths regarding the spirit world and the energy of the universe. Explaining in simple terms to my students how the energy worked, had always been a priority to me and, after the flashback into my powerful former life, I understood why.

Another understanding that dawned upon me at this point, was the fear that consumed me, when I realized one day, at secondary school, that I had the ability to move objects - in anger. I had had a schoolgirl row with my best friend Lorraine and we had been ignoring each other for a few days. I was upset and was at the point where I desperately wanted to make up with Lorraine. On numerous occasions, I had tried to talk to my friend but she was not ready to make up. Lorraine had continued to ignore me and after yet another attempt to make things right, Lorraine stuck her nose hoity-toity like in the air and, flounced towards the classroom door with all of our classmates looking on.

I became angry at my so-called best friend's actions; after all I had been trying to make friends for several days and Lorraine was just being stubborn. Frustration and embarrassment had stirred inside me as my friend walked away from me yet again. The frustration and embarrassment turned quickly to anger and as it welled within me, I felt the urge to vent it. A dark grey cloud obscured my vision and it was at that moment, that a door which had for several weeks been leaning against the book cupboard just inside the class room awaiting re-attachment, began to vibrate. With an almighty slam that shook the whole classroom, the cupboard door fell to the floor, untouched by human hands and landed just inches from Lorraine's feet! The sixteen year old, instantly turned to face me, along with the rest of the class and although no words had been spoken and no threats had been made, we both knew that I had been responsible for what had just happened. I was afraid of what I had done. I was aware that it had been my anger that had given the energy to the door in order for it to fall so dramatically, just missing my best friend! But I was unaware of just how the negative energy from inside of me had manifested in such a way so to have had such a dramatic effect upon the door. Unsurprisingly, Lorraine had quickly decided to make peace with me after the event and I couldn't help wondering if maybe fear of what I could do had prompted her to make peace! (We remain close friends to this day!)

At home that night, I analyzed the events of the day and was afraid; or more accurately I was afraid of my own power. Even though I did not understand how I had done what I had done, I vowed that I would never allow it to happen again - that I would never let my anger manifest in such a way. When Abu visited later that night, I told him that I did not want to be able to harness the energy of the universe and use it in that way ever again. And so the deal was done, it was that simple. I had sent out to the universe a message that I only ever wanted to tap into and manipulate positive energies in the future and that was enough. My intention was enough. The universe heard. I slept easily in my bed that night; but little did I realize at the time, that I had passed a karmic test that day and had learned an important lesson!

****

When I returned from France I decided that I wanted to record all that had occurred and so began writing. Eventually it became evident that I was meant to write a book. Week after week as I sat at my laptop, the words tumbled onto the page and quickly began forming into chapters.

The following summer I went to the New Forest with my own family, my brother's family and my parents on our annual vacation. Whilst in the forest Annie asked me if I would like to accompany her to visit a lady who made and sold oils for a company called Ripple, who were based there. Annie had met the lady at the same festival of mind, body and spirit in Kent that she and Carol had 'bumped' into David. I agreed eagerly to go with my mother always enjoying the opportunity to meet other people with an interest in spiritual things.

Horses in The New Forest

In a beautiful little village, in the heart of the New Forest National Park, Annie and I found the address we had been given for

'Ripple' Limited. The SatNav took us down a leafy, unmade-up road that was dotted with muddy potholes - an unlikely location for an outlet we thought. Eventually we came to a set of black iron automatic gates. Having parked the car, we walked up a winding pathway that led to a building about the size of a large static caravan. The building housed 'The Ripple Shop' and was nestled in the immaculately manicured garden of a large detached house.

My mother and I were welcomed into the building and after purchasing what we wanted, we began talking to the lady, Debbie, who made the aromatherapy oils. She informed us that she was intuitive herself and, that in a dream-state she was 'given' the blends for the oils. She told us how the oils would be able to help people in specific areas of their lives; mainly in dealing with their emotions. In the course of the conversation, I mentioned that I was writing a book. Debbie then informed me that the person, who owned Ripple, was in fact the famous author Anne Jones and that she was sure, after hearing the content of my book, that she would love to meet me. With that, Debbie disappeared, shortly to return accompanied by Anne. All four of us chatted and I, for the benefit of the author repeated the outline of my story. Anne appeared impressed and gave me her contact details, promising to assist me in any way that she could. Before we departed, Anne made me promise to send her the manuscript once completed so that she could advise me on how to go about getting it published.

I was overjoyed - I knew that my story was powerful, but hadn't dreamt of actually having it published! On returning home, I immediately sent the manuscript to Anne. For months following, I heard nothing and so assumed that Anne considered it not to be the right material for publishing. Then, out of the blue, whilst driving home one evening, my mobile phone rang. It was Anne Jones.

"I have read your book," she said excitedly, "It is fantastic - it must be published!"

Anne told me to let her know when I was next in the forest, because she would like to meet with me again.

Following the conversation, plans commenced for our family to return to the forest that summer for our annual vacation together. Before long, the summer arrived and I found myself en-route to the New Forest again, this time with the added excitement of meeting up with Anne. As the group sat down for breakfast on that first day, we looked at the information leaflets that the guest house offered and began picking out places where we all wanted to go. The boys quite fancied Beaulieu National Motor Museum and as that didn't interest Annie or I we decided to make it the day that we paid Anne a visit. The arrangements were made and that morning both groups set off in different directions.

Annie and I arrived in Burley a little early and so decided to take a look around the shops before going to see Anne. We had only browsed around one or two shops when I received a phone call from my brother, Russ. It seemed that no sooner had they arrived at the entrance of the attraction, when our father had been violently sick. Consequently, Russ was taking them all back to the guest house as we spoke. Of course Annie wanted to go to her husband and so she and I cancelled the meeting with Anne and headed straight back to the guest house. Poor Alan had gone straight to bed and fallen asleep, but Annie felt that she had made the right decision in returning to the small hotel.

By the evening Alan was much improved and, by the next morning was back to his normal self - although he settled for tea and toast instead of the full English breakfast he would usually have enjoyed on holiday. The strange thing was that no-one else in the party was taken ill as one would have expected if he had been suffering from a 'bug'. As we had all eaten the same things the day before Alan was unable to identify what had caused his sudden sickness.

Everyone in the party knew how important my meeting with Anne was and so we decided to go to Burley that day, hoping that she would have time in her busy schedule to see us. Burley, Anne's home, is a beautiful village that as well as offering several quaint shops and tea-rooms is also the place from where the Forest Wagon Ride goes. From Burley one could also take a tractor-trailer ride through a deer enclosure or sample cider at the New Forest Cider Farm. Therefore, knowing that the children would all be kept amused while Annie and I disappeared to see Anne, we all set off.

On arrival at the village, the children first wanted to go on the tractor-trailer ride through the famous deer enclosure at Burley Manor. As we had half an hour before the rescheduled meeting, I sat with my brother on the five-bar-gate, at the entrance to the enclosure, to wave everyone else off on their ride, while Annie went to use the public toilets. As Russ and I sat on the gate waiting for

Annie, basking in the sunshine, a lady came running towards us, shouting something about someone having fallen over in the toilets.

Without stopping to think, Russ leapt over the gate and ran to assist hoping it would not be his mother. He was closely followed by me. When Russ neared the conveniences, he barged through the crowd that had gathered to find Annie unconscious on the ground. After a few moments she gained consciousness and wanted to stand up. Her son led her the few yards to the parked car and sat her in the front seat. Annie was disorientated and small speckles of blood were escaping from a graze on her forehead. Annie automatically raised her hand to where she felt the pain most in her head, to see if she could detect a lump. As she brought her hand back down, she was horrified to find that she also brought a clump of hair with it. In order to ascertain what could have happened, Russ retraced her steps and found that a clump of Annie's hair was still firmly attached to the outside brick wall of the toilet building. Annie had no idea of what had happened as she had never fallen before!

We all tried to make Annie go to the hospital to get checked out, but she assured us that she was fine. She had however, developed a pounding headache and just wanted to go home and lie down. Again disappointed, we had no choice but to cancel the meeting once more with Anne. I began to feel as if something or someone was trying to put a stop to the meeting and wondered what the reason could be. Anne was an author who was going to help me to publish my book and I could see no reason for us to be kept apart!

Anne was busy for the next few days and so a meeting could only be rearranged for a few days' time. Thankfully everyone was well on the day and I employed all my driving skills as I nervously drove through the forest to Anne's house, not wanting to tempt fate or give cause for the meeting to be cancelled for a third time. Anne was very pleased to see us and welcomed us in like old friends. As we sat in the lounge waiting for Anne to make refreshments, we acquainted ourselves with her beautiful Labradors. During tea we discussed my book and, after Anne had given her feedback we spoke of publishing possibilities.

The subject then deviated as Anne explained the workshops she facilitated all over the world. It became apparent that she was also a healer and that she took her healing energies out to those in need. In addition to all her other commitments, she told us that she ran a charity 'Hearts and Hands' in which she establishes projects to help the vulnerable in Africa and India. As the conversation continued, Anne told Annie and I that she was a channel for universal energies and that she is able, through her seminars, retreats, CDs and videos to bring forward enlightening and powerful healing experiences. She said that she assisted in healing, empowering and self-development through the sharing of these energies, as well as her own spiritual insights and experiences.

As Anne spoke, my eyes became fixated on a corner of the room; the room began to fade away and a faint high-pitched ringing sounded in my ears.

"OH, not now!" I thought frustrated as I identified the familiar feeling.

Annie recognised what was happening as I sat transfixed. Anne glanced towards her. It seemed that she also knew what was occurring. The spirits were attempting to communicate something to me. Relenting, I mentally agreed to the request for my attention and opened myself to their vibration. As I did so, I found the message was not one of words, but of emotions and the overwhelming one of fear! As I focused upon the emotion I tried desperately to understand it. Then abruptly a snapshot of myself as the powerful magician flashed across my mind.

"Did you know that in a previous lifetime, you were very powerful and you used your power in the wrong way?" Anne broke into my experience.

This was a lifetime that Anne could not have known of through reading my manuscript; Annie knew and, in that moment she became aware that Anne was indeed linking into her daughter.

"You were punished for it!" Anne continued "You were punished by someone much, much, more powerful than yourself and than those whom worked with you."

Now Anne also was sitting staring into nothingness, receiving insight from the spirits.

"I see you on an altar. You and some other men are kneeling before someone!" Anne went on.

Anne and I were linked on the same vibration and I was able to clearly see what Anne was describing. I knew what Anne was saying was true because I was there too – not merely visualizing it – I was living it! I saw myself and the other five men kneeling in front of a man. We were beside the font that I had seen in other flashbacks.

The new man to the scene was similarly dressed to me and was seated on an oversized stone armchair. It was obvious to me that he was of great importance. I knew that the temple in which we knelt was once again packed with people. My people, who had gathered to see my fate and that of my co-workers,

"He is standing now..." continued Anne, as if afraid herself of what she was about to see. "He is towering above you now... And a servant of his has passed him a whip!"

I saw the whip – I saw the handle first, it was shiny, firm and straight and made of leather strips bound together and secured at the end into a rounded projection. The other end was akin to an equestrian lunge whip, if not a little less lengthy. I saw the servant look down, as if fearful himself, as he passed his master the instrument. I knew intuitively that this was a grave situation. A hush filled the large temple and each member of the audience bowed their heads. The feeling that emanated from those gathered was of forgiveness, they all bizarrely seemed to be silently begging for the pardon of those resting on our knees upon the altar.

"Oh my GOD!" exclaimed Anne in a tone that alerted me of some impending doom. "He has cracked his whip over your head!"

At the same time as Anne announced the event; I had seen it! I also saw the spark that flew towards me at the same time, yes just as Anne described it, it actually occurred and she too heard the loud CRACK that echoed around that building somewhere in time. I knew that wherever that moment existed in history, what had been done there had been carried out in order to inflict my co-workers and I with harm.

"You had a curse put upon you. You all did!" Anne announced.

"I know!" replied I horrified. On some level it made perfect sense.

"You had a curse put upon you in that lifetime for all the evil that you did and you have carried it forward with you all this time." Anne finished.

It seemed to me that Anne was just as surprised by the events of that sunny afternoon in the quaint village in England as I was. I thought that my book was complete and yet as we three sat in silence, I realized that once again my fate, the curse, had been down to HIM, the one who had abused me in this lifetime. The evil version of myself, the magician who had manipulated the universal energy to my own ends, was the result of what HE had made me.

The evil man, the man who placed fear in the hearts of his people and had ultimately been cursed for his actions - was in fact Hassat!!!!!

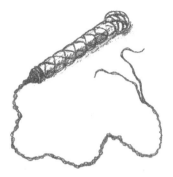

Chapter Thirteen

Closure

13

Anne broke into my thoughts.

"I would like to invoke the universal energies to do a healing for you," she started. "But only if you would like me to?"

I looked towards Annie for reassurance, although I knew that it was an opportunity that could not be missed. I knew that powers of good had fought to bring me to this place, this person, this moment, while it was also obvious that the forces of evil had fought to stop me from reaching this point. I realized that my father's sudden bout of sickness and my mother's fall were attempts by unseen powers to stop the meeting from taking place. Yet against all odds, I WAS here and Anne had offered to conduct a cleansing ceremony for me. The time must be right I thought, or Anne would not have been able to tune into the past with me and hence offer me the opportunity to move on from the past.

Annie gave a nod of assurance and I asked what was to happen next. Anne asked me to sit on the seat that she had placed in the centre of the room and I silently did as was instructed. She placed my hands in my lap and as Anne rested her hands gently on my head, I felt warmth as I was engulfed in white light. Anne then began talking to me and then speaking to the version of myself who had, somewhere in time, been cursed.

On the journey back to the Guest House, I tried to tune into myself to see if I felt any different following the ceremony. Annie and I discussed what had occurred and tried to make sense of it. I knew from my own experiences at Anne's house that my new friend was sincere. She knew from the difficulties that we had incurred trying to arrive at the meeting, that other forces had been involved. Several things were blatantly obvious to me following the realization that it was Hassat that had grown into the evil magician; the first was the fact that it was Hassat around whom my Journey Therapy had been centred. The next thing to be made clear to me was the answer to a question that had often bugged me. I had always known Abu to have been the father of Hassat yet I could never understand why, even though I had had many incarnations since that of the young boy, he had chosen to guide me through this lifetime. The obvious answer was that he felt that he was in some way to blame for the man that Hassat grew to be and therefore the consequences. I also deduced that that must have been one of the reasons that my mother – 'the jean clad lady' had also wanted to be present.

The final conclusion I made was that my drive to become a scientist and to work in the laboratory that arose when I was about eight years old, must have originated from my experiences as Hassat. He had been forced to murder people by mixing deadly potions, whereas in my position as microbiologist within the laboratory I worked, I had had to check medication and their ingredients to ensure their purity. In that role, I was responsible for ensuring the safety of those who were to take the medication. Was that, I wondered, a means of settling my karma?

The return journey was thought provoking and both Annie and I were exhausted when we arrived back at our temporary accommodation. After reacquainting with our family we were soon rejuvenated and ready for our evening meal together.

****

A few years passed and I thought little about my manuscript. One day, I assumed, it would be the right time for it to be published and I was sure that I would know when that was. Meanwhile, I continued to pursue my spiritual development, using the understanding I had gained of who I really was and of how past versions of oneself have an effect upon the here and now. In addition to running workshops and courses I arranged for a variety of speakers to attend the centre from where I worked. One such speaker was Matt Selley, a PhD in Metaphysics, and he sparked much interest. One of those interested was an ex-student of mine – Tina, whom I had befriended. Tina lived in Essex and wanted to attend the talk and so I offered her a room for the night at my house. My offer was accepted and we began planning our weekend. We decided that we would use the day following the talk to catch up on each other's development. Tina had recently been on another Merkaba course and I was keen to learn about her experience.

The talk was enlightening and I made a mental note to book Matt again for the following year. The next morning Tina and I settled in the lounge for our long overdue chat. We were looking forward to the opportunity of spending the time to explore each other's development, as it had been some time since we had last met up. We relished the 'me-time' and covered much ground before I brought up the subject of Merkaba. I asked Tina if she had experienced any of her past lives using the technique. Tina nodded and began relaying the snippet of the lifetime that she had experienced.

"I know I was in Egypt," Tina began, "all I saw was myself as a male. I am in some sort of temple. I am at the front of the temple and I am standing over some men. There is some sort of stone bowl thing beside me…"

As Tina paused, I began to have a flashback from the scene that I had experienced a few years before at Anne's house. And as Tina continued to describe her experience it suddenly became clear – it was apparent that Tina was in fact the person who had cursed me!

"It was YOU!" I exclaimed, "Oh my God, it was you!" The realization came without emotions.

As the words left my lips, the room began to swim, both of us commented upon it. Then a shrill noise penetrated our ears and it seemed that we were both being transported somewhere else.

"I feel really strange," said Tina.

"ME too," I replied holding my head as if to steady it and keep myself in the present.

Both of us realized that we had once experienced something very serious together and that Tina had determined the fate of me and the others in that lifetime who worked with me. I knew that Tina had once inflicted a grave curse upon me. I also realized, in that moment, that Tina had had no choice; that she had acted in the best interests of those over whom I had exuded such negative power. At that moment both Tina and I realized that for our souls to move on, we needed to meet in this lifetime and more than that, that we needed to become friends. It was only now that we were firm friends that our past could be revealed to us and harmony could be restored as we overcame a grudge that had bridged centuries.

I explained quickly the gist of my book and the relationship that I had had with my abuser throughout time. It seemed that as my story unfolded, Tina realized that each person has a history, something that makes us who we are. That day Tina realized that in the lifetime of yesteryear, I had behaved the way I had because I was forced into it. And that was enough; it was enough for Tina to understand. Nothing more was necessary. On a deeper level, Tina was able to understand and let go! It was as simple as that – no flash of light – a simple understanding on her part was all that was required.

Out For a Meal With Tina

After the strange experiences of the day, we decided to go out for a meal. We continued our spiritual conversations over dinner and when the discussion turned back to what had happened earlier; we both experienced the same feeling of disconnection with the here and now again. We heard again the shrill noise and, the table and chairs in the restaurant appeared to be moving. We both found ourselves transported back to the scene somewhere in our past, this time with a sense of detachment – as if the events of that fateful day somewhere in history no longer mattered.

"Oh my god," exclaimed Tina, "it has been a really strange day!"

"Yes!" I agreed "It has been a very strange day!"

We knew exactly what had happened! Closure! Simply, closure!

Chapter Fourteen

The Conclusion

14

A wise person once said: –
"It is the journey that is of greatest importance and not the destination!"
As I reflected upon the strange experiences that had occurred over the last few years I added the following to my journal:

'I have been rich (Edwardian lifetime), I have been poor (the street urchin), I have been attuned to nature, living an idyllic lifetime hurting no-one (Indian lifetime). I have taken from others in order to create material wealth for myself, hurting many (The Gang of Thieves), I have given to others, sharing my knowledge in order to create spiritual wealth (this lifetime). I have killed and been killed. I have been powerful and powerless. I have experienced exactly what my soul needed to experience in each incarnation. And my soul is grateful. I am grateful – for everything!
'I have not been judged for my good and bad deeds, by a vengeful GOD. I have followed my destiny, and in doing so I have been encouraged, guided and loved by my spirit friends. I have been privileged in this lifetime to be able to access my soul and to peer into alternate incarnations and that has allowed me to gain an understanding of myself in the here and now. It has allowed me to set myself free from the Karmic baggage which previously restricted me.'

****

Many years ago my friend Brenda put an idea to me that I have thought about many times since. She said that every relationship we have in our lifetime is not necessarily as simple as it seems and she went on to tell me this parable: –
Jesus was in heaven and had gathered all his best friends around him. He looked about and said: –
"My life plan is written; I have chosen and we have agreed which of you are to be my parents and my family. We have decided who of you are to be my disciples. There is just one more thing to be decided upon!"
With that Jesus looks around the room,

"I need someone to betray me!" he stated.

A hush descends and each person not already allocated a role in Jesus' next incarnation, bows their head in an attempt not to catch his eye.

"Oh, come on," Jesus pleaded, "One of you must do it!"

He looked around the room, stopping to point at each person with their head bowed in turn. Each adamantly shook their head. When Jesus had asked every one of them the all-important question, he looked down disheartened.

"Look," he continued determined, "You are my best friends; won't one of you please help me? I have taken great pains to prepare my life's journey but if I can find no-one to betray me, it has all been in vain. My life will be worthless – without meaning!"

He turned to face a small, inoffensive looking man in the corner and reaching out his hand to him he pleaded once more,

"Judas, you are my very best friend. Please will you do this for me?"

Judas hesitated and then seeing the need Jesus had for him to play such an important role, he agreed with one stipulation.

"OK Jesus, I will do this awful deed for you, on one condition – that as soon as it is done I am able to return home!"

"It is a deal!" Jesus joyfully agreed and the heavenly contract was written.

When the time came, many earth years later, in the Garden of Gethsemane, Judas kept his promise to his best friend and betrayed him with a kiss... Minutes later he took himself back to the heavenly realm.

****

From that parable, it is easy to see that all life is interconnected; that we are, on some level, either in a past or present lifetime connected to many of those around us in a deeper more meaningful way; a web that is more intricate than we could ever hope to comprehend. Sometimes those who appear to harm us in this incarnation, may in fact be our best friends or, as in my case had originally been my best friend. The experiences I have shared with you in this book, have taught me that we all experience a variety of aspects of life during our many incarnations. That being the case, it would not be right for you to abandon all idea of developing your spirituality in this lifetime because, if you are reading this book hen that is exactly what you are supposed to be doing in this incarnation! Fate has placed this book in your hands - so it is time, my friend, for you to take another important step along the pathway we call the journey of life!

I would like to leave you with a simple quote that my father gave to me many years ago when, as a child, I was to receive an injection and was feeling afraid. It is a quote that I have repeated to myself and others when life has been difficult and is one that I hope will help you by nature of its simple truth: -

"Soon you will be looking back on all this!"

I have journeyed through the turmoil of many lifetimes during which I experienced love, hatred, pain and suffering, fear, freedom, power and powerlessness, separation, loneliness, family bonds and loyalty, death, destruction, murder and evil beyond words. Now, as myself in the here and now – as Wendy, I am looking back on... The Journey of a Lifetimes!

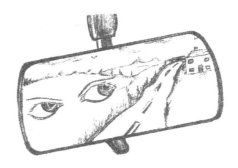

The End

What is Bliss?

When I was falling into the 'pit of despair' I trusted the energy of my own emotions and allowed myself to fall – going with the experience I was having. A Tibetan Buddhist Master Chogyam Trungpa in his book 'Glimpses of the Abhidharma' (published by Shambhada Dragon in 1975) states when discussing energies that relate to emotions: -

'Both liberation and confusion are that energy, which happens constantly, which sparks out and then goes back to its basic nature, like clouds emerging from and disappearing into the sky.' (Page 11; 1975)

He later goes on to explain how bewilderment, another energy form is responsible for sometimes causing us to panic. He suggests: -

'If the energy were to go along with its own process of speed, there would be no panic. It is like driving a car fast; if you go along with the speed, you are able to manoeuvre accordingly. But if you suddenly panic with the thought that you have been going too fast without realizing it, you jam on the brakes and probably have an accident. Something suddenly freezes and brings the bewilderment of not knowing how to conduct the situation. Then actually the situation takes you over rather than just being completely one with the projection...' (Page 11; 1975)

It seems that when I fell into the 'pit of despair' the trust that I had, kept bewilderment and panic at bay, thus enabling me to manoeuvre accordingly, without panicking and therefore allowing me to be at one with the situation I found myself in.

'Totally giving up', according to author and spiritual teacher Jean Kline is, 'Letting go of ego – stripping away what society has made one, this allows one to – in that moment – to be fully conscious.'

We are, after all, products of our culture, parents, schools, friends, religion and everything that makes up the society in which we live. Only when the layers formed by years of indoctrination are stripped away do we become fully conscious in our own right – this is real birth or rather the birth of the real you!

Once you have experienced this freedom, you cannot and, never will, return to who and what you were. The birth of consciousness is referred to by many as bliss - although often the term is used flippantly nowadays. In my story I allowed myself to fall into the 'pit of despair' where I gave up, let go of ego, allowed the layers that society had levied upon me to fall away and, in that moment became conscious. I found bliss.

It is my hope, dream and desire that you now seek your own true bliss!

What's next?

During a trance demonstration after I had completed this book, I was told that 'The Jean-Clad Lady' the mother of Hassat, was actually incarnated on the earth at this time and that is why she arrived at the camp-fire dressed as she was. During the trance session, I was informed that 'The Jean-Clad Lady' and I, were due to meet. I look forward to the destined meeting with the excitement of what it may bring and also the possibility of another book to follow!

I am also in the process of writing a book called 'Madness, Mayhem and Mediumship' about my spiritual experiences from the age of two, which accelerated when my family moved into a haunted house and I discovered, to the amazement of my friends, that I had the ability to move objects with my mind, in addition to seeing and hearing spirits!

Following the remarkable journey that led me to the discovery of my past lives and of how they constantly impacted upon my current life, I decided to study it and became a Past Life Regression Therapist and Hypnotherapist.

The time is right for me to use my experiences to enlighten and therefore help others!

That is the reason that I have published this book. Although I do not just want people to read about how past lives impact upon current lives, I want to help people to experience that for themselves. I therefore, offer my services as a Past Life Therapist and Hypnotherapist in order to take the next step of my life's journey.

Who knows, there may even be the makings of another book using my clients' experiences!

I also am considering writing a workbook for those who are searching for Spiritual Awareness & Personal Development.

Contact Details

I now teach Reiki, Self-Awareness and Spiritual Development, including meditation, relaxation, stress management, thought organization, and many other positive life-skills techniques.

In 2013 I completed training as a regression therapist myself!

I run my own classes under the name
'...one step at a time...'

To contact me and to find out more about my classes, workshops or Past Life Regression Therapy please email

onestepatatime@sky.com

Or visit

https://dealspiritualcentre.wordpress.com/

Live Your Life

And

Be Free!

Your new life commences now.
Live it well, make wise choices and follow
your soul's destiny.

Bibliography

1) Brandon Bays, The Journey, (published by Element Books see recommended reading)

2) www.journeytherapist.com/journeytherapy

3) Chogyam Trungpa, Glimpses of the Abhidharma, (published by Shambhada Dragon in 1975)

Recommended Reading

1) 'The Journey' by Brandon Bays (published by Element Books ISBN-10: 0722538391)

2) 'The Field' by Lynne McTaggart (published by HarperCollins ISBN-10: 0060931175)

3) 'Your Souls Plan' by Robert Schwartz (published by North Atlantic Books ISBN 978-158394272-7)

4) 'The Ancient Secret of The Flower of Life' by Drunvalo Melchizedek (published by Light Technology, US ISBN 9791891824172)

5) 'My Ever Best Friend' by Charles Cane (published by Courtney Publishers ISBN 10: 0956720102)

Websites you may find helpful in your spiritual quest

Brandon Bays The Journey
www.thejourney.com

Robert Schwartz
www.yoursoulsplan.com

Lynne McTaggart
www.theintentionexperiment.com

Merkaba Meditations
www.ascensionnow.co.uk/star-tetrahedron-merkaba.html

Past Life Regression
www.pastliferegression.co.uk

Anne Jones
www.annejones.org

Jane Clark
www.thewellnessstore.co.uk

"There are two ways to look at life. One is as though nothing is a miracle. The other is as though everything is!"

Albert Einstein

Printed in Great Britain
by Amazon

79451272R00099